A Happier Life

How to develop genuine happiness and wellbeing during every stage of your life.

by Shar Khentrul Jamphel Lodrö

Edited by Dr. Adrian Heckel

TIBETAN BUDDHIST RIMÉ INSTITUTE

Belgrave, Australia

ISBN: 978-0-9944453-2-2 (paperback)
ISBN: 978-0-9944453-3-9 (e-book)

Published by:

THE TIBETAN BUDDHIST RIMÉ INSTITUTE

This work was produced by the Tibetan Buddhist Rimé Institute, a not-for-profit organisation run entirely by volunteers. This organisation is devoted to propagating a non-sectarian view of all the world's spiritual traditions and teaching Buddhism in a way that is completely authentic, yet also practical and accessible to Western culture. It is especially dedicated to propagating the Jonang tradition, a rare jewel from remote Tibet which holds the precious Kalachakra teachings.

For more information on scheduled activities or available materials, or if you wish to make a donation to support our work, please contact:

Tibetan Buddhist Rimé Institute Inc.
1584 Burwood Highway
Belgrave VIC 3160
AUSTRALIA

www.rimebuddhism.com
temple@rimebuddhism.com

Contents

Acknowledgments

I dedicate the virtues of this book to my parents who brought me into this world and took great care of me—I can never truly repay their kindness. I am so happy and grateful to have had the opportunity to write this book because I am still quite new to the English language and culture, and my experience living in a western country is somewhat limited. I am, therefore, extremely grateful to those who have contributed and assisted in the development of this book, not only in making sense of my poor English but also in discussing and contributing ideas. I would like to thank Dr Adrian Hekel for his enormous assistance in creating this book, which was beyond editing. I believe Adrian's intention and motivation was genuine and unconditional. I hope that as you read this book you appreciate Adrian's efforts, as without him this book may not have been completed. I would also like to express my gratitude to Julie O'Donnell, who helped me start this book and provided endless support, generosity, dedication and loyalty. Every opportunity I have had to work on this and other projects is thanks to Julie's kind support, so I cannot thank her enough and will never forget all her help. I would also like to acknowledge and thank all of the individuals who contributed to this book, especially Stephanie Davis, Mark Cleary, Lisa Jobson, Dorothy Welton and Kristy Peters. May you encounter good fortune and further your spiritual development.

Khentrul Rinpoche
Melbourne, Australia
July 2015

Editor's Preface

I first met Khentrul Rinpoche six years ago. At this time he was a new immigrant to Australia—he knew only fragments of English and knew almost no-one. Yet in our clumsy attempts to communicate I discovered that he had a story to tell that was quite remarkable and his training in Buddhism was second to none. When he mentioned the idea of writing a book on happiness several years ago, it took me a while to be convinced that we could write something that was original and practical, yet after some time, I realised that although many of his ideas were quite simple, the depth of wisdom behind them was quite profound.

At the same time as I was working on this manuscript, I completed my training as a doctor and worked for a little while in general practice. This work was like a magnifying glass into the inner world of everyday Australians. It was an opportunity to witness the heartbreak, suffering and misery that people go through every day, yet also the amazing joy and resilience that some possessed in the face of the most trying of circumstances. As well as my own life experience, working as a doctor convinced me that happiness does not 'just happen' by chance and it is certainly not a trivial matter. It is without doubt something that we should think about deeply. After all, what else really matters?

In addition, through my work as a doctor I noticed that many people seemed to ignore the reality of suffering, death and dying. They often regarded spirituality as a private matter or had not really thought about deeper issues all that much, being so focused on getting on with life. I therefore felt a book like this could help people come to know how spirituality is embedded in the experience of daily life, not as something separate from it. Perhaps it could also serve as a 'bridge' for those who have grown up in Western culture and are interested in the 'spiritual life'.

In editing this book I hope my style of writing and the additions I have made have not trivialised or tarnished the wisdom that Khentrul Rinpoche has tried to convey. In order to make the book more accessible, I have tried to cross-reference his ideas with some of the latest research in psychology (as detailed in the notes section). Much of this is based on my experiences at the international Happiness and Its Causes conference in Sydney, as well as my training in medicine and conversations with mentors with great experience in counselling and psychology. I hope that these additions will not detract from the essential message of the book, and I accept blame for any errors or omissions.

Finally, I wish to dedicate my contribution to this book to my parents, who have always been there for me unconditionally. Also, I genuinely wish that reading this book will help make some difference to your quality of life.

Adrian Hekel
March 2010

CHAPTER ONE

An Introduction to Happiness

You might wonder why someone like me would be interested in writing a book about happiness. I've never been to school, I have no university degree and I have had very little exposure to the information and technology of the modern world. Instead I have lived most of my life as a simple monk, isolated from the rest of the world in the remote mountains of Tibet.

When I reflect on my life, however, I realise that I have been through an amazing variety of experiences which have actually given me quite a good grasp of what is really essential and important in life, so much so that I could not stop myself from wanting to explore the question of happiness and to share with others what I have learnt. My heartfelt wish was to write a book about happiness that would explore every aspect and every step of life in a way that was unique and useful to everyone, whether they are young or old, religious or non-religious, rich or poor. I wanted to write it in such a way that reading it carefully, reflecting on its contents and putting into practice certain exercises could actually change how happy you are.

When I look back on my life and recall the relationships I have had, the decisions I have made and the lessons I have learnt, I can only think how helpful it would have been to have had a guidebook or manual on how to lead a happy and contented life. I would have felt so fortunate to have the opportunity to read a book like this. This is why I decided to write this book, thinking that I am now in a position to share a few of my insights on how to deal with the challenges we all face at different stages of life and what true happiness really is.

Almost everyone assumes that we cannot find happiness in the face of hardship and unfortunate conditions. I have slowly learned that this is indeed possible, as I have been through many challenging times, yet from a young age I have never really been that unhappy—in fact I'm probably happier than many people with an easy life. As a child I was denied a position of high social status and instead lived a harsh life, herding yaks in the mountains in temperatures as low as minus thirty degrees. When I was a teenager I found intense happiness in romantic love which I felt would last forever, yet after my father died I made the tough decision to sacrifice this, as I felt a genuine calling to honour my parents' wishes and become a monk.

As I began monastic life at a comparatively late age, I found it difficult to become accepted and adapt to this completely new way of life. I was competing with monks who had been trained full-time since childhood, while I was only a lowly yak herder. Later on I found it quite difficult to adapt to the culture and lifestyle in Australia, where I knew absolutely no-one and could speak only a few words of English.

My many years of authentic Buddhist training, as well as my rich and diverse experiences living in the modern western world, have opened my eyes to the fact that happiness does not depend on the conditions people usually associate with this. I have been fortunate to gain a deeper understanding of happiness, in that it can be attained amidst hardship and misfortune rather than being dependent on a comfortable life. When I reflect on my own experiences, I now realise that it was the difficult times that taught me to be happy, giving me inner strength and a renewed appreciation of many things.

When I arrived in the West, with its totally different culture, lifestyle and way of thinking, to my surprise all the understanding I had gained about happiness was reinforced. Rather than changing my perspective, the views I held were enriched and deepened. This occurred after meeting and talking to many western people over these last few years, as well as being able to closely observe life in the West and learn a little about concepts of western psychology, philosophy and science. I have tried to weave these insights into the text with the hope of making the profound wisdom of the Tibetan Buddhist tradition more accessible (references for each chapter are presented at the end of this book).

I hope this book will be like a mirror through which you can see the whole of your life—the past, the present and the future. Although you may be young, you may find the chapters for older people useful. Alternatively, you may be quite old but identify most with the initial chapters for teenagers and young adults. I also share my background in the Buddhist tradition throughout this book. I hope that some of you will find this useful, especially if you are curious about the idea of a 'spiritual life', which is often misinterpreted by people in the modern world. I pray that this book will assist you in some way, to plan for and commit yourself to living a happy and meaningful life, whatever religion or belief you may follow.

WHAT IS HAPPINESS?

What is happiness? Is it just about feeling good or excited, having a comfortable life and having our desires met? I believe these can all be features of happiness, but really it is much more than this. When we use the word *happiness*, we are often not aware that it is a vast and profound subject. This one word cannot adequately describe the limitless levels of happiness.

On the surface, happiness might include physical comfort, mental excitement or momentary feelings of pleasure, as well as feelings of love and acceptance. At a slightly deeper level, it could also include being fully engrossed in a particular activity or the process of striving to achieve a particular goal. A happy state of mind does not necessarily come with achieving goals, but rather during the process of enthusiastically moving toward them. At each of these levels, and within each level as well, different degrees of satisfaction or contentment are felt.

From a deeper perspective again, a degree of happiness comes from understanding that failure and loss are a natural part of life. With this understanding, we can use all circumstances as a learning ground to discover a happiness that comes from within, despite all the ups and downs. This leads to a sense of equanimity and inner peace, with an increased ability to control our emotions. Many spiritual and non-spiritual philosophies:

1. Recognise that there are many levels of happiness
2. Appreciate that happiness can exist in any situation

We often only see one of these levels. If we genuinely recognise and appreciate its many dimensions, the door will open to understanding and realising the deeper levels of happiness. This understanding leads to a limitless potential for happiness which is much greater than any we may have ever been aware of.

What does it mean to 'accept' the darkness in our lives? Generally we fall into two extremes—on the one hand we ignore the suffering that is part of life, and on the other hand we can become completely fixated upon this suffering. In the first instance we are shielded from the realities of life and are taken by surprise when something unexpected happens, such as the loss of a job or the death of a loved one. In the second instance we are fixated on this dark side, falling into depression, negativity or resigned acceptance, and fail to appreciate the many bless-ings which life brings.

Thankfully there is a middle way, a vantage point from which we can be aware of the suffering and yet be aware of the blessings at the same time. We could lose all our wealth or even a close friend, yet still appreciate what we do have, such as our health and a good mind, and that we are blessed to live a life where so many things are provided for. Happiness and contentment can therefore only arise when we genuinely appreciate the light side of life while also understanding that the dark side is natural and so are not overcome by unfortunate events. We can only truly appreciate life if we are aware of both its fulfilling and 'suffering' natures.

Understanding the darkness in our lives increases our compassion, as we realise that all beings undergo the same struggles as we do. We can then produce a deep desire to be kind and to develop unbiased, unconditional love and compassion, reducing the tendency to think only of our own self-interest. This brings us to an even deeper level of happiness, spurring us on to devote our lives to something greater than ourselves.

Finally, the deepest and most profound level of happiness is the discovery of the innate 'selfless nature' which lies at the core of our being. This is a constant source of joy and unbiased love, totally independent of outside circumstances. In the Buddhist tradition we call this our 'enlightened nature', which we can unveil by eliminating every trace of self-interest.[1] We then uncover our true potential to be fully happy, gain complete control over our emotions and naturally benefit others.

Modern psychology also speaks of different levels of happiness. According to Martin Seligman, sometimes known as the father of positive psychology, there are three basic levels.[2] Firstly, there is the moment to moment feeling of pleasure that we all strive for, then there is the joy which comes from being absorbed in a particular task or the process of achieving a particular goal and finally, there is the deep sense of purpose and fulfilment which comes from knowing that life is profound and meaningful, which can be further enhanced by developing key virtuous qualities.

Although we each have different ideas about what happiness means to us, these different levels apply to us all, regardless of who we are. Understanding happiness in this way can give us a much richer appreciation of its ultimate potential and power. I will talk about how to find these different dimensions of happiness throughout this book. My hope is that each of you will relate to this and be able to apply it in a way that suits your personality type and current level of understanding. I will, however, emphasise cultivation of the deeper levels, where true fulfilment which is based on compassion and altruism can be found. If we can find this within ourselves, we will have discovered a depth to our being which is a constant source of joy, peace, contentment and courage, regardless of life's ups and downs.

IS HAPPINESS ACHIEVABLE?

Every living being has an innate desire to achieve some degree of happiness, no matter what their position in life or how old they are. Some people may be disillusioned and choose unwise means for achieving happiness. For example, some people may physically or emotionally harm someone thinking, in their ignorance, that this will bring them satisfaction and happiness. Regardless of how people think they are going to achieve this, it is important to realise that the search for happiness and satisfaction are indeed the ultimate driving forces behind everything we do. This is a natural fact and there is no point investigating why we have this desire. It would be like trying to analyse why fire is hot or water is liquid and therefore wouldn't really help us.

However, what is absolutely necessary is that we examine whether or not happiness is achievable. Do we all have an innate potential for happiness? Is it dependent on causes and conditions? And if so, what are the right causes and conditions? Or is it 'fate', something which just happens when things 'fall into place'?

To answer the first question, yes, we do all have the innate potential to achieve happiness. Every belief system throughout the world, both theistic and non-theistic, will tell us that happiness is not just random or a product of good or bad luck. Furthermore, the idea that we each have a fixed potential for happiness that cannot be changed all that much is being challenged.[3] Both the experience of traditional spiritual cultures and modern scientific research are showing that, if we cultivate happiness diligently and skilfully, we can definitely achieve it.

In the world today and throughout human history, there is living proof that numerous people have attained a high level of happiness. This has often been the result of significant struggle or hard work. We know this from their testimonies and the testimony of others, and we can see this in their actions. There are a select number of people we may even call 'enlightened'. Without exception they point to the same innate potential for enlightenment residing equally in all of us.

Secondly, we posed the question: is happiness dependent on causes and conditions or is it just random or 'fate'? Yes, happiness is completely dependent on causes and conditions. If we look at the history of human civilization, and if we thoroughly investigate our own experience, we will find there is nothing which does not rely on causes and conditions to make it occur. In the same way, it is impossible for happiness just to arise randomly.

At the observable level we all agree that nothing occurs without particular causes. Similarly, the *way we perceive things*, including all the thoughts and emotions that pass through our minds, also depends on particular causes and conditions. This is why we can speak about happiness in the same way.

THE RIGHT CAUSES AND CONDITIONS

If happiness is definitely achievable, we have to ask ourselves what the causes and conditions are that will bring it about. This is by far the most important question and the one that requires the most extensive answer. I will give a brief outline now and then address this again in later chapters.

Firstly, we should ask ourselves if the majority of human beings are genuinely happy. If we reflect honestly the answer must surely be 'no'.

Even though we may appear to be happy, there is often an underlying feeling of dissatisfaction, or that 'something is missing', or we may be easily shaken when something unexpected happens.

Most people think that 'if only they had that much wealth', or 'if only they were healthy or beautiful', or 'if only that relationship would work out', *then* they would be happy. This way of thinking leads us to limited happiness through physical comfort, mental excitement, momentary feelings of pleasure or being accepted and loved. We may not even notice that we can spend an entire lifetime relentlessly pursuing things like wealth and social standing.

Unfortunately, by thinking this way we mistake the conditions which bring momentary comfort or pleasure for happiness itself. We may be so focused upon these secondary conditions that we get trapped in a narrow view, unaware of the primary conditions. It is important to distinguish between:

- Primary conditions—your attitude
- Secondary conditions—money, relationship, health, beauty

For example, we may not appreciate the genuine happiness to be found through being fully engaged and immersed in an activity that we find meaningful. We may overlook the happiness and contentment which comes from gratitude and enjoyment in simple things.

At a more profound level, happiness depends on how deeply we understand life and all the circumstances we face. A wise outlook allows us to see that we cannot expect life to be easy or successful, or that we will necessarily gain something through hard work. We believe that we can strive hard and achieve what we set out to do, whatever our definition of success is, yet do not generally allow for everything not going to plan. Even if we fail, however, it is still important to strive, and there may be a substantial underlying benefit from our efforts. If we are able to reflect carefully, we can be much better prepared to accept the worst, whatever misfortune or sorrow befalls us.

Furthermore, we can be aware that the true goal of this lifetime should be to focus on developing unbiased compassion, helping others and learning to accept ourselves for who we really are, rather than holding onto an image of ourselves that we try to live up to.

This naturally leads to a state of mind where we are no longer dissatisfied and our self-cherishing is greatly reduced. Self-cherishing doesn't mean we are a particularly selfish person. Rather it means not considering others as important as ourselves or putting ourselves before others. Putting ourselves first is a normal, deeply engrained habit, and considering others to be equal to ourselves usually requires diligent practice.

Finally, the most powerful and true cause of happiness is the ability to develop genuine loving kindness and compassion in an unbiased way. Such a state of mind is the true foundation of happiness for everyone, regardless of their circumstances. We discover that focusing on other peoples' happiness will naturally make us happy, while being concerned only with our own happiness can lead to disappointment and failure to achieve what we expect. If you attain the deepest level of love and compassion then wherever you go you will feel at home. You will be able to hold a deep level of compassion and tolerance for everyone you meet, regardless of their attitude and actions, feeling completely at ease and relaxed.

Usually, even if we have some form of kindness and compassion, it is still limited or partial, being associated with some degree of attachment, egotism or self-cherishing. If, on the other hand, we develop love and compassion in an unconditional way, our happiness can become so powerful and secure that feelings like sadness, depression, loneliness and even stress have much less chance to arise. Ultimately, the basis for this unconditional type of compassion is our enlightened or innate 'selfless' nature, and even limited compassion brings us closer to this.

THE IMPORTANCE OF THE MIND

Nothing is either good or bad but thinking makes it so.
— *William Shakespeare* —

∽

In the same way as we think that our happiness relies on external circumstances, we can also fall into the trap of believing that unhappiness is determined by external conditions. We might blame our unhappiness on the lack of money, or we may have enough money but work too hard and don't have the time for a holiday. We can blame our boss who doesn't respect us, or our partner who doesn't love us enough. However, it is not external events that cause our unhappiness, it is our minds.

When I began writing this book I had just moved into a new house. We felt we'd paid more than we should have and a few days later the hot water system failed, meaning we had to survive with cold showers in the middle of winter. It was easy to be annoyed and mope around feeling sorry for ourselves. Upon reflecting on our circumstances, however, we were able to view the situation from a different perspective. We realised we were actually very fortunate to possess a home of our own and to have running water, as many people in the world do not even have clean water to drink. By looking at our problem from this new perspective and appreciating what we had rather than what we didn't have, we were able to see just how minor a misfortune it was.

This example is really quite trivial compared to many of the challenges we have to face. To give another example, recently the most beloved person in my life, my dear mother, passed away. On top of this, several people to whom I had been very kind and who I trusted deeply, tried to harm me despite my best intentions to help them. At first I was extremely shocked. It felt as though my whole world had been turned upside down, that I had lost everything and that my entire life's work amounted to nothing. However, when I considered all the worse things that could have happened, I realised my situation wasn't actually that bad. I still had my health and my integrity, I still felt safe and I still had people around me who cared about me and would look after me.

When I reflect on some of my other experiences, I can appreciate that misfortune often brings unexpected opportunities. If we allow ourselves to see situations in this kind of positive light, we can then benefit greatly by practising gratitude. This particular situation, for example, taught me some significant lessons about myself that I can apply in the future. It has also strengthened some of my relationships with those close to me.

If we learn to view things from a different angle, we can then appreciate all that we do have, like running water, and know that not having hot water for a short time is really not such a big deal. We can also learn to realise and accept that misfortune is a natural and inevitable part of life for all of us. At first something may seem like misfortune but it may actually teach us some valuable lessons. In this way, a friend turning against us, the death of a loved one or the loss of something we have worked hard towards will not necessarily cause us to be unhappy. Even though we may feel intense sadness, if we can learn to accept difficult situations while maintaining a steadfast and balanced outlook, then we will experience far less misery.

As His Holiness the Dalai Lama explains, fundamentally the true causes of happiness can be found in our minds:

Granted, external circumstances can contribute to one's happiness and wellbeing, but ultimately happiness and suffering depend on the mind and how it perceives.

UNDERSTANDING SUFFERING AND ITS CAUSES

The great philosophies of nearly every culture lead us to a common idea, that when we look honestly at our situation we must come to the conclusion that happiness is not an innate or natural state of life—so it is just as important to accept the 'dark' as it is to appreciate the 'light' of life. Unfortunately, it is very easy for us to think we have a 'right' to achieve true happiness, and we therefore expect to find it. This outlook, however, will always lead to disappointment.

The first step to achieving happiness is to know that suffering is an inescapable part of life. Look around you and think of all the people you hold dear. Every second, from the moment they are born, they are getting older and approaching death. We don't know who will have a long life or a short life. This includes you. Sickness and death can come at any time without warning and even with the best medical care in the world there is nothing we can do about it. Nearly all of our experiences contain some element of suffering—not getting what we want, getting what we don't want, parting from the people we love or perhaps loving someone who doesn't really care that much about us. We may even just have a general sense of dissatisfaction that we can't pin down, causing us to question all the conventions held by those around us. Good circumstances are also destined to change, no matter what stage of life we are at.

We can understand that suffering is inevitable when we admit that, even though we strive hard from birth to death, we are never able to find lasting happiness. If life did not contain this inherent suffering, but instead was 'neutral', then most people would find genuine happiness since everyone is pursuing happiness from birth to death. However, this is not the case and it is rare to find someone who has actually achieved genuine happiness, therefore if we do find some sort of happiness, instead of taking it for granted we should learn to really appreciate it, even be amazed. We should realise that finding happiness in a life pervaded with suffering is like finding a waterfall in the middle of a desert!

However, I am not saying that since suffering is such an inescapable part of life we just have to accept it as our fate because there is no way to overcome it. If we are sick, we consult a doctor who tells us why we are sick and gives us some medicine which hopefully will help. In the same way, if we recognise suffering for what it is we can think deeply about the causes and conditions that lead to suffering and happiness. We are often so fixated on the happiness or suffering we are experiencing that we are convinced it is due to good or bad luck. We rarely consider trying to identify the cause with a view to changing it. Therefore, the wisest thing to do is to look at the root or source of the problem, like a doctor identifying the cause of a disease.

This leads to the question of what the root cause of all our suffering and dissatisfaction is. Since happiness and suffering are not directly caused by external events, as we often think, but rather by *how the mind reacts* to external events, we could say the source of our suffering is rigid or unwise thinking. Whenever we fail to accept what is happening around us, we become locked in a cage of negative thoughts and emotions like anger, greed, pride, jealousy or fear. These emotions take control of us, reinforcing our negative thoughts. This cycle will go on and on until we are finally able to let go of these negative emotions and replace them with more wholesome, positive ways of thinking and feeling.

Another way of saying this is that suffering and dissatisfaction depend upon how stubbornly the mind holds onto its expectations that life will unfold in a particular way. As we tend to place so much importance on external events, we either become attached to them or push them away, and this attitude is what limits our level of happiness.

Knowing this, is it then possible to achieve lasting happiness? The answer is a definite 'yes' because happiness depends on causes and conditions, as I have already discussed. In particular, it depends upon the cultivation of a wise, flexible mind that is not weighed down by expectations, along with wholesome thoughts and actions such as impartial love and compassion. This true compassion evolves naturally once we develop qualities such as ethical conduct, diligence and wisdom.

Since happiness and suffering both depend on specific causes, if we abandon the causes of suffering and embrace the causes of happiness, we can be completely confident that we will become happier and eventually reach an inviolable state of lasting happiness. We will then become like a deep ocean which remains calm underneath no matter how rough the waves are on the surface. Although it is not an easy task, if all the causes of suffering are completely eradicated, then unhappiness is no longer possible! The purpose of this book is to learn how we can overcome the causes of suffering while cultivating virtuous actions in order to reach this state of ultimate happiness. How we can accomplish this is explored throughout each chapter.

ANCIENT WISDOM, MODERN WORLD

We can further deepen our understanding of the true causes of happiness by looking at some insights contained within western and eastern philosophy, and also by probing the discoveries of modern psychology and neuroscience.

What I have discussed so far is significantly influenced by my perspective as a Buddhist monk, however many of the great western philosophers also tell us that to find any kind of happiness we must accept the reality of suffering[4] and realise that wiser thinking could help us overcome it. Seneca, tutor to the decadent Roman Emperor Nero, saw firsthand the consequences of anger and pride. Based on his experiences, he spoke of the danger of having unrealistic expectations, which make us think that many things are unfair or disappointing and thus lead to frustration and suffering.

Socrates, who claimed that an 'unexamined life is not worth living', emphasised the importance of using logical reasoning to question assumptions we often hold, such as 'being rich will make us happy'. Epicurus, meanwhile, proposed that the causes of a happy life emanate from companionship, simplicity and living a well-analysed life; too much focus on seeking pleasure would always lead to dissatisfaction.

Modern psychology agrees with these general principles. Many people in our community suffer from depression. One method for treating depression is cognitive behavioural therapy,[5] which tries to help people become aware of their negative thoughts and perceptions and then replace them with more rational thoughts which more closely reflect the reality of a situation. For example, we may think we are unworthy if we make a mistake, and this assumption makes us forget that nobody is perfect and that our sense of worth really comes from within. This kind of therapy can help some people with depression just as effectively as medication, and can be used to overcome a variety of unhelpful thinking habits born from destructive emotions like anger, guilt and anxiety. It enables patients to recognise their negative thinking habits, and the discipline of regular mental training can then help them overcome negative thinking and see the reality of their situation more clearly.

Although modern psychology has mainly focused on understanding and treating mental illness, in recent years there has also been much research into the factors which make us flourish and achieve a much higher level of happiness. This field of 'positive psychology', which focuses on how to cultivate positive mental states, has revealed that there are three crucial components to happiness: pleasure, engagement in life and finding a meaning or greater purpose to life. Of these three components, research has shown that pleasure is by far the least important cause of a happy and satisfied life. There are quite a few skills we can practise to increase our sense of engagement and meaning, such as keeping a 'gratitude journal' or acting generously in the presence of others.

Of the large number of psychological studies that look at the question of happiness, I would like to mention one that is particularly interesting (carried out by Philip Brickman in 1978). Many people dream of winning the lottery and think that if they won all that money, happiness would be theirs! However, psychologists who studied lottery winners found they were generally no happier[6] one year after winning than they had been before. People who had become paraplegics through some kind of accident were also interviewed. I would agree without doubt that this is a terrible thing to happen, and indeed most of the paraplegics admitted that in the first month after their accident they had thought at least once of killing themselves, however, one year after their accident, most of them were as happy as they had been prior to becoming a paraplegic; in fact, most were as happy as the lottery winners were one year after winning the lottery. This study clearly shows that neither happiness nor unhappiness depends upon external conditions. Happiness comes from within ourselves and is dependent upon how we perceive our situation.

Do scientists believe that achieving lasting happiness is possible for everyone? Neuroscientists have found that the brain has an incredible ability to change when we train ourselves to think in a particular way, known as neuroplasticity. Experiments have shown that if a person pays close attention to what is seen or done, the areas of the brain that receive visual signals or register motion will become larger. For example, if we spend many years playing the violin, the area of the brain that controls finger movements[7] will enlarge. Similarly, if we spend a large amount of time focusing on love and compassion[8], many areas of the brain, especially in the left prefrontal cortex, will change. Most scientists used to believe that everyone had a 'happiness set point', a certain level of happiness which we couldn't really change once we became adults.[9] Now, with the benefit of much new research, scientists are discovering that the brain can be transformed at any age.

Therefore, we should be able to train ourselves to increase our level of happiness, no matter how old we are, as long as we know the conditions which are necessary for a happy life.

CHAPTER TWO

Exploring the Conditions of Happiness

We all have an innate potential for happiness, yet we have to be aware of the specific conditions which will lead to the discovery of this potential. We have mentioned that happiness depends on the mind rather than external events, and furthermore that it depends on many causes and conditions related to how we think and act. We will now look carefully at what these core conditions for happiness are, which apply regardless of a person's lifestyle or their stage of life. To begin with, we will explore the question of basic human needs.

BASIC HUMAN NEEDS

First of all, we must acknowledge there are certain basic human needs which, for most of us, must be met before we are able to contemplate the higher dimensions of happiness. Certain very highly developed individuals can attain happiness regardless of external conditions, such as some yogis, lamas or hermits who live in the Himalayas. They still attain happiness despite an often meagre supply of food, very basic shelter and a lack of human contact, sometimes for many years. This is only accomplished through years of diligent spiritual practice. Most of us, however, require the following needs to be met:

1. **Survival Needs**

   This includes things such as food, water and shelter. Without these, most people find it impossible to focus their minds upon higher pursuits.

2. Safety

Despite the fact there are no assurances of complete safety no matter where we are in the world, we must have basic shelter from the elements—protection from fires and storms, for example—as well as safety from being harmed or killed by other beings.

3. Contact and Communication

If we wish to participate in society in a meaningful way, we have to have some form of communication with others. This can be with other people directly or through the written word. Communication enables us to learn and provides us with guidance. Without communication it is extremely difficult to achieve something which affects or benefits society, regardless of our goal.

4. Freedom

It is crucial to understand that there are different types of freedom— external and internal. Happiness is still possible even without external freedoms such as freedom of speech or the ability to access health care. The absence of these freedoms, however, would make it more difficult to achieve the things that may be important to you. On the other hand, inner freedom, which means freedom from our own emotions and desires, is absolutely necessary for happiness. I will explain more about this later.

5. Recognition and Respect

I am not referring to fame or celebrity, rather recognition from others that you are an individual and that you are respected as an autonomous human being. This means that you are not simply regarded as an object or a commodity. If you live in a democratic country, you most likely have already been granted the rights and respect of an individual human being.

If each of these fundamental needs is met, the potential exists for us, along with everybody else, to achieve great happiness. Though it may seem surprising, we do not actually need anything more. If we are already fortunate enough to have these basic needs met but fail to recognise or appreciate them, we are failing to make the most of the precious opportunity we have to become a happy person. Pursuing anything more may help us become happier, yet our endeavours may also backfire and make our situation more complicated or lead to frustration.

NEEDS AND DESIRES

The five basic needs mentioned above are necessary for both survival and for attaining favourable conditions for happiness—both externally and, more importantly, internally. In fact they are essential for happiness. However, these basic needs only have to be met in a basic way, and we therefore have to be able to discern the difference between needs and desires. What do I mean by this? By striving for luxury and trying to hold on to more and more external things, we can experience some pleasure or satisfaction, but we gradually lose our inner focus and therefore find it harder and harder to be truly happy.

We can survive with just water, bread and some vegetables, but instead we usually want many different varieties of drink and food. We can keep warm with only one or two modest outfits, but instead we may buy a whole wardrobe of fashionable clothes to bolster our self-image. For shelter and protection, we often seek the luxury of a house with more rooms than are really necessary. The pursuit of other material things, such as the latest model car we have dreamed of for years, may well create more difficulties and lead us away from happiness.

We also have so many different ways to communicate and gather information—mobile phones, the internet, television and newspapers, just to name a few. As we have become accustomed to many of these things, we can easily grow dissatisfied if our expectations are not met. Furthermore, many of us are caught up in compulsively striving for what we consider to be a better life, working long hours and even getting ourselves into debt to finance this 'better life'. If we instead made the choice to simplify our lives and accept a lower income, we could have more spare time to devote to the kind of things that would give our lives a far greater sense of meaning.

Often we are not content to just be recognised as a human being, instead wanting to be considered someone special, above others. We seek love and acceptance, and we want to be held in high regard by our partners, family, friends and our community, wishing to be thought highly of by those we care for. On top of this, we have a very powerful impulse to fall in love, which for most of us is mixed with great attachment. This can lead to jealousy, resentment or even heartbreak if things don't work out the way we expect. We therefore need to be really honest and always remind ourselves that there can be great sorrow lurking in the shadow of romantic love, and we may not always need it in order to be happy.

Although we may think that money will make us happy, this is not necessarily the case either. Granted, we need money for survival, but what we think is enough depends on our attitude. Many of us know wealthy people who are much less happy than those with modest incomes, and the case of the lottery winners mentioned above seems to support this.

Therefore, whenever we find ourselves wanting more money or being unduly tempted by material possessions, or caught in the grip of almost any desire, it is important to reflect upon the question, what do we really need? You will soon discover you will be happier in the long term if you understand the difference between needs and desires and then simplify your life accordingly.

PLEASURE VERSUS HAPPINESS

Often people think that happiness implies a feeling of excitement or pleasure. We experience excitement, for instance, when we purchase our first car or house, get married or go on a holiday. We experience pleasure when we pursue our favourite hobby, go to the beach or the movies, or spend time with friends. We may mistake this momentary feeling of pleasure with happiness. However, this kind of 'happiness' is by its nature brief and deeply unstable, as it relies purely on an external stimulus. When this external stimulus is taken away, this feeling of happiness disappears.

Although there is nothing wrong with experiencing pleasure, it is crucial for us to be aware that this is only the most superficial level of happiness. Being addicted to pleasure will prevent us from accessing the deeper dimensions of happiness.

A more stable type of happiness is that which comes from the attainment of mental ability and cultivated aptitudes. This includes the satisfaction gained through pursuits such as scholarship, science, sport, art or religious practice. It may also include making a new invention or engaging deeply in something we are committed to. This is similar to the type of happiness we experience when we are in a state of 'flow',[10] which occurs when we are completely engaged in our work or an activity we enjoy. This occurs when we are so absorbed in what we are doing that there is simply not much chance for boredom to arise. Because we enjoy it, and we are good at it, there is far less chance for sadness or anxiety.

Both of these types of happiness are more stable than that which relies entirely on external sensations because they arise in part from within and are reliant on our mental attitude. However, these types of happiness are still not entirely stable. For example, what if the scholar loses access to resources for any reason? Or the scientist is unable to continue his research through a lack of funding? If this is a person's sole source of happiness then they may well be plunged into despair.

Again this confirms that true happiness does not rely on any form of external stimulus or condition. It is completely stable, as it is a feeling that comes completely from within—a feeling characterised by wisdom, compassion and the knowledge that life is profound and meaningful. If we have genuine compassion and wisdom such qualities are always within us and are independent of external conditions. This does not mean, however, that we should refrain from activities which give us momentary pleasure, rather that we should ensure that everything we do is connected with a deeper sense of meaning and purpose. A person with this knowledge can reach a stage where he or she is no longer dependent on the influences of the outside world. A person with this kind of happiness is completely free.

WHOLESOME MENTAL QUALITIES

We have mentioned that no matter how good our external conditions, we will never be truly happy unless certain wholesome mental qualities are present. These mental qualities arise deep from within one's heart and, when cultivated, form the basis of a mature, deep and rich character. These qualities, aligned with what we value most in our lives, are what we would wish to be remembered for. They also support and give our lives meaning in challenging times.

The essence of these wholesome qualities is supported by nearly every major religious and cultural tradition in the world. Regardless of the tradition, there are varying levels of understanding or maturity with which we can embrace and practise these qualities. It is important to remember that, rather than a goal, these mental qualities describe a direction that we desire to keep moving in. For example, if you strive to be empathetic and caring towards others, this is an ongoing commitment that will shape how you live for the rest of your life. It is not something you attain and then forget about.

If we commit ourselves to cultivating wholesome mental qualities, we will be connecting with our deepest values and will therefore always have some degree of happiness and meaning in our lives. Each time we put these wholesome qualities into practice, we can be confident that a seed will be planted that will eventually ripen into true happiness. It is useful to think of the cultivation of these qualities as a process of cause and effect—a good seed will lead to a good result, while a bad seed will lead to a bad result. Certain people will find that some of these qualities come more naturally to them than they do to others. This is similar to the idea of 'signature strengths' in modern psychology,[11] which describe good character traits that can help us create a rich and meaningful life if we choose to focus on them.

The wholesome qualities we must cultivate are divided into direct and indirect categories. Indirect qualities contribute to our happiness by improving our external conditions in some way, whereas direct qualities will immediately lead to happiness. Although difficult, it is still possible to be happy without the indirect qualities, but we can never attain happiness without the direct qualities.

Before we detail just what these qualities are, it is necessary to mention the importance of wisdom and compassion. Wisdom is a combination of all the qualities I have listed below and is a part of them, yet also stands above them. Wisdom is not however, the same as intelligence, as it does not mean knowing a lot of things. Rather it is having a good, practical understanding of what is truly important and how to apply this in daily life.

Compassion, too, is absolutely necessary if we are interested in attaining the highest levels of happiness. Practising each of the other qualities will lead us to a certain level, but it is only through cultivating a genuine spirit of compassion or altruism that our ultimate potential will be uncovered. Above everything else then, we need compassion and wisdom to attain happiness.

While practising these qualities, it is likely that our attitude and actions will be appreciated, affecting those around us in a positive way. However, the reverse can also be true and we may find that some people respond negatively. This is because we are walking a path towards self-lessness and those who are not walking a similar path may feel threatened or fail to understand where we are coming from. Their reactions could be challenging and unreasonable if they cannot see the purpose of what we are doing. This situation calls for us to develop still more compassion in order to understand the source of their negative reactions, and to respond in the most skilful and appropriate way. It can then become an opportunity to practise our spiritual discipline in everyday life.

A. Indirect qualities

Strength of character

If we have a strong or courageous character, we can achieve many things in our life and attain enjoyment and satisfaction as a result. A person who lacks a strong character will have difficulty making decisions and achieving goals, and therefore will find happiness much harder to come by.

Ambition, enthusiasm and determination

These are qualities which allow us to achieve many things in life. If we have no clear direction or enthusiasm we will fall into complacency or laziness and never improve our own or others' situation in life. Our life may therefore become very boring. Even if we have ambition, if we lack a strong will or determination it is easy to get distracted and waste our precious time. Remember, however, that working hard does not mean that our life will be harder; things will actually be much easier in the long run.

Although some people may get overly stressed if they are too ambitious, it will place us in a much better situation than being lazy, and we will gradually come to enjoy the process of working hard each day, especially if our goals are meaningful. When ambition is combined with a good heart and wisdom, we can be guaranteed of positive results in the future. Without a warm heart or altruism we may achieve great things, but the consequences may be negative if we are not careful, as we have seen historically with the rise of dictators who have caused great harm.

Thoughtfulness, caring for others and empathy

These qualities help us to create and maintain good relationships with other people, which is important for our own happiness. Additionally, we will find that if we are kind to others, there is more chance that others will be kind to us—sometimes straight away, or sometimes many years later. The merit of our actions will certainly increase, maybe even in a hidden way, and the beneficial results will naturally come. No-one can achieve complete happiness without helping others.

Respect for others

If we always have respect or consideration for others then we are sure to have fewer problems in our relationships with people, and we are far more likely to maintain peace and tranquillity. Respecting others means acting with humility and courtesy, and being willing to understand their point of view or empathise with their limitations, which naturally leads to feelings of closeness, affection and harmony in relationships.

Patience

This is an important quality, but it is easy to misunderstand the way in which patience should be developed. If we can change a situation for the better by taking action then it is not good to sit back and think, 'I will just practise patience here'. This kind of attitude is a form of laziness or complacency, not patience! Having patience means we can handle or cope with any situation that is not going well and be tolerant, no matter how frustrating it may be; yet we should still have the presence of mind to act skilfully and appropriately rather than just 'giving up' or waiting without bothering to search for a solution.

B. Direct qualities

Self-control

This is absolutely necessary in order to manage our emotions, especially negative emotions such as anger and jealousy, unless we have an exceptional ability to use these emotions constructively. In some cultures, people tend to suppress true feelings and emotions for fear of appearing rude or impolite, and then over time these suppressed feelings can overflow uncontrollably. They may then react with severe emotional outbursts or by withdrawing completely and walking away from any challenging situation, which is much worse than a normal exchange of emotions. The key point, therefore, is to train oneself to accept and contain the healthy and normal flow of emotions rather than suppressing it. Emotions we can learn to control include anger and sadness (which can spiral into depression if left unchecked), as well as unrealistic expectations or desires such as uncontrolled emotional love.

Gratitude

If we feel gratitude for the things around us from one moment to the next, then it is almost impossible to feel depressed or unhappy. Most of our unhappiness arises not from misfortune but from lack of gratitude, as this stains our perception of the outside world. Without gratitude we can never be happy, regardless of our circumstances.

Appreciation

This is closely linked to gratitude, since if we are grateful we will naturally be appreciative. Usually people are unhappy because they forget to appreciate the many good things they have in life. Some people choose to view the world from a distorted perspective in which everything appears negative regardless of what is actually happening. Without appreciation we will not attain true happiness. It can therefore be very beneficial to train ourselves to appreciate any good fortune or opportunities that come our way, no matter how small they may appear.

Contentment

When we experience happiness we experience satisfaction. This sense of satisfaction does not depend on external conditions or prosperity, but rather on the inner quality of contentment. Without this quality we will never be completely satisfied—we will always feel that we need more. We will also feel that others are better off than us, leading to a spiral of harmful emotions such as jealousy and greed. To cultivate contentment, however, is to cultivate happiness. Some people naturally have some degree of contentment and therefore it is easier for them to develop this quality, while others may need to be more diligent. Nevertheless, it is definitely something we can all learn to build and nurture.

Humility

A humble attitude helps us learn to respect others and cultivate close relationships. Like an open container or an open door, it allows many other good qualities to come our way. Pride and arrogance, on the other hand, are like an upside-down container or a closed door, as they make us think or act rigidly and shut us off from learning new things. Humility is therefore essential if we wish to learn from others, respect others, get along better and gain a clearer, more compassionate view of reality.

C. Direct and indirect qualities

Self-worth and self-confidence

These qualities are indirectly responsible for happiness, as they are necessary for achieving goals in our life. Additionally, if we feel good about ourselves our mind is automatically happier! Therefore, sometimes even small things, such as wearing nice clothes or getting a haircut, make us feel better about ourselves and may contribute to our self-confidence.

Focus

If we are able to have strong focus and pay close attention to everything we do, we will find it easier to train our mind in all the other qualities. By being mindful or paying attention to what is actually happening in the present, we will not be distracted by unnecessary thoughts or mental chatter. Furthermore, we can learn to experience a state of 'flow' or absorption in many of the activities we undertake, leading to increased joy, efficiency and also productivity. The more successfully we can maintain a state of inner calm, the less anxiety we will experience. Over time, our mind will become clear, sharp and strong.

Forgiveness

Forgiveness is directly linked to happiness. If we learn to cultivate genuine forgiveness then our minds cannot be disturbed by anger or resentment. This promotes a sense of inner peace. Forgiveness is also indirectly responsible for happiness, for when we sincerely forgive people our relationship with them is sure to become more harmonious.

Forgiveness is similar to patience in that it must be applied wisely. It never means letting people walk all over us. In any situation in which someone does us wrong, although it is crucial to always hold an attitude of forgiveness, we can still actively try to improve the situation. Forgiveness also does not mean that we suppress feelings such as anger—it is essential that we first acknowledge any anger or resentment we may feel, as only then can true forgiveness occur.

Generosity

The indirect effect of generosity is an improvement in our relationships with others. Additionally, when we have a generous attitude and give others our time, energy, advice, material belongings, or indeed perform any kind of generous act, there is no way we can feel unhappy at the same time. Our heart becomes warmer and we become more peaceful and happy. We must remember, however, that being generous to others should not compromise our ability to love and take care of ourselves. It is vital to have a strong sense of self-worth and self-love as a basis for extending love and generosity to others. Without this we will be limited in how much we can share with others.

Compassion

Compassion is essential if we are to lead a genuinely happy life, and the methods for developing it are explained in detail throughout this book. Compassion is caring for other people and for ourselves in a wise way, with a strong awareness and recognition that we all equally wish for happiness. True happiness can never be attained if we seek it at the expense of other people, yet it is certainly attained through having compassion for others. It is crucial, however, that this begins by cultivating compassion and caring towards ourselves, and this includes such things as eating well, exercising and setting aside quiet time to 'recharge our batteries'. We cannot possibly be compassionate towards others if we do not know how to look after ourselves.

When we feel true compassion, it doesn't matter whether we like or dislike another person or whether we find them intelligent or unintelligent. In the same way that we want ourselves to be happy, compassion means you also want *them* to be happy, recognising that all others have this same desire. This has both a direct and indirect impact on our happiness. When we display genuine compassion, especially without expecting anything in return, our actions towards others will be kind and loving and our relationships with them will almost certainly improve. But more importantly, our own mind will be clear and calm, like a bright summer sky without a single cloud. True happiness can never be attained if we seek it at the expense of other people, yet it is certainly attained through having compassion for others.

WHOLESOME ACTIONS

So how do we develop these wholesome qualities? It is not enough purely to sit and think to oneself, 'I must be grateful, I must have self-confidence', day after day. Our thoughts guide our actions, but at the same time our actions have some influence on how we think and on the situations around us. Sometimes we may not have the experience or the wisdom to know how to act in a certain situation. I have therefore provided specific guidance on how we can live life based on *wholesome actions* throughout this book. Acting in a cultivated and mature way, with our actions guided by a foundation of good ethical conduct, will lead us to a more wholesome mental attitude and make the mind a more fertile place for happiness to grow.

As we grow older and the circumstances of our lives change, we will be faced with many different challenges, so I have provided specific guidance for the types of challenges which are generally experienced at the different stages of life. Underlying all of this advice, however, are some basic concepts or rules by which to live a good life. These five rules (or 'Five Precepts', as we call them in Buddhism) are taken directly from the teachings of the Buddha. However, they are reflected in almost every moral and religious teaching throughout the world and provide a good moral framework for how one should live (although their interpretation can be complex at times!). These five rules are:

1. Not to kill

This means we should not intentionally kill or harm any living being, including such creatures as mosquitoes, ants or spiders. Every living being has feelings such as fear, and we are therefore called to respect and protect all forms of life. This also applies to recreational fishing, which can cause fish to experience immense pain and stress simply for the sake of personal pleasure.

2. Not to steal

This means we should not take the wealth or property belonging to others without their permission and we should only take that which is freely given without manipulation.

3. Not to lie

This means we should not lie or cover up the truth for our own benefit or in defence of our own self-interest.

4. To avoid sexual misconduct

This means we should abstain from engaging in immoral sexual conduct which leads to harmful consequences for ourselves and others.

5. To avoid harmful intoxicants

This means we should not indulge in intoxicants such as alcohol or other drugs, knowing that they cloud the mind, damage the body and lead to self-harm or harm to others.

When we speak of wholesome actions, this also includes things we should do to look after ourselves in the best possible way. In the same way that we should avoid harming others, we should also avoid harming ourselves by failing to pay attention to our diet, over-eating, having poor sleep habits or neglecting to exercise. In Tibet most people have quite a harsh life, so they tend to get plenty of exercise during the day and adhere to a good diet, with obesity being almost unheard of. Yet in the West we are often born into a sedentary lifestyle where exercise and healthy eating are optional, and often we are too busy to make time to look after this area of our lives.

There is no question that exercise is beneficial for our physical wellbeing, though now we know it is crucial for mental wellbeing as well. A recent study, for example, concluded that exercising three times a week is as helpful for some patients with depression as taking an antidepressant.[12] Moreover, those who were just on the drug were much more likely to relapse into depression than those who exercised. In addition, other studies have shown that regular physical activity leads to reduced anxiety, better sleep, improved mental functioning and increased self-worth.

As a Buddhist, I also believe it is a fact that our day to day actions, or karma, contribute to the events which happen to us in this life and in the next life. Although you may not share this view, I feel it is important to mention such ideas as I believe they can benefit everyone. Even if you are not familiar with the idea of karma, it can still be helpful to understand how the enjoyment or frustration that we experience fundamentally depends on how we treat each other.

OVERCOMING UNWHOLESOME STATES OF MIND

While we need to cultivate and adopt wholesome mental qualities, it is equally important to recognise and abandon negative or unwholesome states of mind. These are the principal obstacles to achieving genuine happiness. These unwholesome qualities essentially stem from a lack of wisdom. They include:

- Low self-worth
- Excessive fear or anxiety
- Lack of self-control
- Apathy
- Complacency
- Discontentment
- Miserliness or greed
- Pride and arrogance
- Denial
- Selfishness
- Intolerance
- Impatience
- Hatred or resentment
- Uncontrolled anger
- Ingratitude
- Cynicism.

In the long term, these unwholesome states of mind will always lead to an increase in the suffering and dissatisfaction we experience. We should therefore try, as best we can, to identify and overcome them. Although rooting out our negative tendencies is not an easy task, it is definitely achievable if we work skilfully to overcome them.

How, then, can we do this? Firstly, if we train ourselves diligently to focus on positive qualities, especially gratitude and compassion, unwholesome qualities will gradually subside. This can be likened to a skilled carpenter knocking out and extracting a coarse peg by using a fine one. Furthermore, we can reflect deeply upon the dangers or disadvantages of unwholesome qualities, reminding ourselves that they always result in suffering for ourselves and others.

Although training our minds in this way may be harder, for example, than losing weight, a commitment to this kind of work will be much more beneficial in the long term. As our minds become more peaceful and stable over time, the unwholesome tendencies will gradually subside and good qualities such as love and courage will shine through.

Many of us will find it difficult to overcome strong emotions as they are so firmly rooted in our subconscious minds. These emotions and impulses are like a shadow that is always there with us, even though we are not aware of its presence. They are often connected to difficult events in our lives which we try to screen out, so that particular triggers will be associated with certain painful memories or faulty beliefs such as *I'm not good enough*. They come back to haunt us as unhealthy reactions such as uncontrolled anger, shame or anxiety, like a bird swooping down upon us when it sees its prey. Although these negative emotions and impulses are, to an extent, a normal part of the human condition, the good news is they are definitely able to be changed.

What, then, can we do about these more stubborn emotions? The key is to shine the light of compassionate awareness upon them. Rather than trying to deny, avoid or fight our inner experience of unpleasant thoughts, feelings and memories, which can create much more suffering in the long run, we can first learn to accept them as part of our human condition. We can then see that they do not necessarily have to interfere with our ability to live a rich and meaningful life.[13]

In addition, we can learn to recognise that beneath 'negative' emotions such as anger and shame there is often an intense clarity, fearlessness and a deep sense of caring. With practice we can learn to avoid the extremes of uncontrolled anger on the one hand and a feeling of shame or hurting inside on the other. Both reactions are based on a false perception of reality, yet if we stay with the raw experience or feeling before these reactions take over, we can transform these emotions into an expression of deep caring, just like a skilful doctor who is able to make what would normally be poisonous to us into medicine. We can then choose to engage assertively with our body and speech, while our mind is completely free from uncontrolled anger or false perception, or we can choose not to engage, seeing that this may be the best course of action, without holding onto any reactions such as shame and resentment or simply acknowledging how these reactions used to be triggered in the past.

Often we have long standing assumptions about ourselves and the world we live in, leading to unhealthy beliefs that cause us to experience strong emotional reactions over and over again.[14] This can then be reinforced by a culture which encourages us to succeed, 'move on' and ignore many of the things that challenge us. For example, we may have a preconceived idea of how things should turn out in our life and that everything should go the way we would like it to, or that we are only a good person if certain conditions are met. We might think that happiness will only come if we keep on striving to be the best, win approval from others or make lots of money. Maybe we have the idea that achieving happiness is unrealistic because our situation is so bad, making us discouraged or depressed. On the other hand, we might only have a limited understanding of what happiness is and block ourselves from discovering the deeper levels of happiness. At the most extreme level, we may even think it is impossible to achieve happiness at all!

These assumptions are all obstacles to wisdom and, unfortunately, some may even be reinforced by the people and culture around us. Becoming aware of these assumptions can help us change our way of thinking and learn to accept what is happening rather than continuing to struggle against it. It can also lead to genuine compassion for those going through similar struggles—we learn to touch our 'soft spot' and gain a humble acceptance of the human condition.

In order to challenge these assumptions and be able to genuinely accept who we are, it is important that we speak openly with people we trust. This may include a counsellor, a support group, a close friend or acquaintance with a certain amount of wisdom, especially if they have gone through similar experiences to our own. We should always remember that someone less experienced may be able to help us. Be sure, also, to consult a doctor if you are feeling depressed or are so overwhelmed with day-to-day life that you are unable to function normally.

While we are learning to accept the pain and negative tendencies that are an inherent part of being human, we can also get on with the job of creating a rich and meaningful life for ourselves—and this is the main focus of the rest of this book. In so doing, we will naturally be cultivating positive states of mind, such as altruism, while gradually weakening and eventually transforming our negative tendencies. In this way we can gradually train ourselves to control our emotions, while at the same time accepting their existence and the suffering that comes from their presence. When we are no longer controlled by emotions and have learned to conquer the habit of putting ourselves first, we will finally discover our true 'selfless' nature, the source from which all good qualities naturally come.

HAPPINESS THROUGH THE AGES

The root causes of happiness remain the same throughout our lifetime, no matter what age we are. Everyone has the potential to cultivate their minds in a way that enables the seeds of happiness to grow. The core or direct mental characteristics are of equal importance through every age. The indirect mental characteristics tend to wax and wane in their importance, depending on the stage of life we are at and the goals we are aiming for.

Because every human being has the potential to achieve happiness, regardless of their age, I will discuss the various stages of life and offer some advice for each of these. You can refer to the section that deals specifically with your age group, or you can learn from them all and perhaps pick up useful tips about happiness that you might not have heard about before. You can also try to identify which of the wholesome mental qualities come more naturally to you and focus most on these strengths first. You will then find that many of the other good qualities will begin to come naturally as well.

Before we begin, however, I must point out that happiness requires persistent training of the mind, and for some people this may require great diligence and determination. Just as physicians need many long years of training before they can practise medicine, most of us also need a great deal of training, in both our attitudes and actions, to arrive at the stage where we have a consistent, permanent feeling of happiness. I therefore urge you to think of this book as a precious gem and keep on referring to it whenever you are facing difficulties and yet also when you encounter good times. Remember too that this book is one of many resources and may not necessarily provide the most suitable guidance in your situation. It is wise, therefore, to read other books as well or seek advice from people or organisations that you think may be of assistance.

My hope is that you will be able to remember the advice that applies to you wherever it is presented in this book. It is important to not just be content with an intellectual understanding but rather *apply these teachings in everyday life*. By taking this advice to heart I have great confidence that you will experience a significant difference in your level of happiness.

Sowing the Seeds of Happiness

This chapter contains a few short stories designed for parents to read aloud to their children, or for children to read for themselves if they are old enough. Normally in a children's book we find pictures, photographs and other simple and clear ways of communicating a message, however, as this book is not just for children, there are no pictures, and some of the messages contained within the stories may be more complex than those found in general children's books.

Generally speaking, children are naturally happier than adults due to a lack of major responsibilities and concerns. Happiness is almost always within their reach, and they can play and be joyful without anyone teaching them how. Yet it is most important that we sow the seeds for future happiness at an early age, so that children learn to be wise and find true happiness in adulthood. The following short stories are intended to be like signs on the side of the road, pointing in the direction of a happy life. My wish is that parents will read and discuss them with their children, helping plant the seeds for good qualities which are sure to help them throughout their entire lives.[15]

THE STORY OF CONTENTMENT

Once upon a time there were two children, Jenny and John, who were cousins. Although they were the same age, went to the same school and grew up with the same people, they thought and behaved in very different ways.

Jenny owned many expensive toys. She was very possessive of them and refused to let anyone else play with them or even touch them. Even though she had lots of old toys that she no longer liked or played with, she still refused to give them to anyone else. Jenny was never content and always wanted new things even though she already had so much.

John, on the other hand, didn't have quite so many toys but was happy with those he did have. He was a very easygoing and easy to please boy who always offered to share his toys with other children, especially those less fortunate than he was. John didn't need much to make him happy. When there were no toys for him to play with, he amused himself playing with stones or twigs or whatever he could find.

As the two cousins grew up they kept to their same ways. Jenny was never content with what she had and always wanted something more. She was dissatisfied with her boyfriend, even though he was very kind and loved her very much. She thought she could find someone more handsome and intelligent. Jenny also had good friends and many possessions, yet no matter how much she had, she was never content or truly happy with anything. As she grew older she remained this way, ending up a very insecure, unhappy and lonely woman.

John remained grateful and content with whatever he had or didn't have. He was always relaxed and considerate in his relationships with others. He grew up to be a very happy and much-loved man, with many wonderful friends and a strong, healthy and loving family. Wherever he went he spread happiness. John had been content from a very young age. Somehow he knew that happiness wasn't about having lots of things, but rather about sharing what he did have with others.

Which person would you rather be like and why? Talk to someone about this, maybe your Mum or Dad. How would they answer this question?

THE STORY OF FRIENDSHIP[16]

There was once a magpie which lived in the branches of a willow tree beside a lake. In the waters of this lake, not far from the willow tree, lived a turtle. There was also a deer which would often come to drink at the lake. All three animals were very close friends.

One day when Deer came to the edge of the lake for a drink of water, he was suddenly caught in a trap that had been left by a hunter. His foot was snared by very strong ropes. Hearing his cries, Turtle and Magpie quickly gathered together to discuss how best to help their friend.

Magpie said, 'Sister Turtle, as your jaws are strong and sturdy, you can use them to chew and cut through these ropes. Meanwhile, I'll find a way to prevent the hunter from coming back to the lake.'

And so Turtle began to chew at the ropes while Magpie flew to the hunter's hut.

The following morning, the hunter walked out the door of his hut carrying a sharp knife. Suddenly Magpie appeared and flew into his face with all her might, again and again. Dazed from the attack, the hunter ran back to his hut, but before long sneaked out the back door of the hut. But Magpie was clever and had been expecting him to do this. She swooped down and began attacking him again, striking him hard in the face with her talons. Discouraged by this second attack, the hunter concluded it was an unlucky day and decided to rest, thinking it would be best to try tomorrow instead.

Unfortunately for the three animal friends, the next morning the hunter prepared himself for another attack from the magpie by covering his face with a hat. Unable to stop the hunter, Magpie sped back to the forest to warn her friends.

'The hunter is on his way!' she yelled.

By this time Turtle had almost chewed through the last of the ropes, though the rope felt as hard as steel and her jaws were now bloody and raw. Just as the hunter came into view, Deer gave one almighty struggle and, with a kick, snapped through the last of the rope before running off into the forest.

Angry to see Deer escape, the hunter picked up an exhausted Turtle and placed her in his leather sack, leaving it hanging on the branch of a nearby tree. He then went off to search for Deer.

Concealed behind some bushes, Deer saw the danger Turtle was in. 'My friends risked their lives for me', he thought, 'so now I must do the same for them'. And so, pretending to be very tired, he stepped out in full view of the hunter.

Thinking he would be an easy catch, the hunter began to pursue Deer. When they were deep in the forest, Deer suddenly bolted, running until he was out of the hunter's sight, then covered his hoof-prints and returned back to the lake. He then used his antlers to lift the hunter's bag off the branch and shake Turtle out. Turtle was then able to crawl back into the water and hide, while Deer ran back into the forest.

Arriving back at the lake, the hunter found his bag lying on the ground, empty. Frustrated and disappointed, he picked up his knife and walked back to his hut. He was so discouraged that he thought he might just as well give up hunting—perhaps he could work on his neighbour's farm instead!

Turtle and Magpie had saved Deer's life, and now Deer had surely saved Turtle's life. And what's more, witnessing their friendship and how they had worked together to help each other, the hunter made the decision to give up hunting. Seeing how much they cared for each other made him realise it would be wrong to kill them, just as it would be wrong for him to harm his own friends.

Imagine that you were Turtle in this story. Think about the friends you have made in this life. Who would be Magpie? Who would be Deer?

What does being a friend mean to you? How can you show another person that you are his or her friend?

THE STORY OF SELF-ACCEPTANCE

There was once a young boy called Alex. When he was a toddler, he was trapped inside a house that accidentally caught on fire. He was rescued by two brave firemen just in the nick of time, but had to go to hospital for several operations due to his severe burns. Now he had an ugly looking scar from the left side of his neck all the way down his left arm.

Alex was very shy at school because he was embarrassed by the way he looked. His school uniform did not completely hide his scars, and he was often teased because he looked different from the other children. The other children never thought about how Alex would feel about this.

'Alex the reptile man,' they would taunt him unkindly. He wished he was bigger and stronger so that he would have the courage to fight back when he was teased. Instead, he would just quietly walk away and find somewhere he could be alone, away from the cruel remarks of the other children.

One day the school gardener saw Alex being teased and approached him.

'I can see your life is not easy,' said the gardener, in a voice full of warmth and sympathy. 'Maybe it would help if I share a little story with you.'

Alex nodded.

'There was once a house,' the old man began, 'which from the outside looked like a dreadful, ugly old place. The roof was full of rust and the paint was peeling off the front wall. Even the pipes were rusty and leaked whenever it rained heavily. Inside it was very small and the kitchen area was cramped. It didn't even have a TV.

'However, there was a beautiful cosy fireplace which glowed with a large, warm fire, and a really comfortable couch on which visitors slept the night. Neighbours and many friends would often come and visit. They would stay up until late, huddled around the fireplace, sharing stories and having a wonderful time.

'And so,' the old man finished, 'even though the house didn't look so good from the outside, on the inside it was a much-loved place to be. And this is what really mattered.'

Alex understood. It didn't really matter that he had an ugly look-ing scar and was teased at school, because it was the kind of person he was on the inside that really counted. Soon the children who teased him stopped, because they saw Alex was no longer getting upset. A different group of children then began to play with him and eventually accepted him as a good friend.

Alex had learnt to accept himself for who he was and with that he was able to find an inner confidence. Others would see this and respect him for it.

Have you ever felt like Alex?

Are you able to accept and love yourself just the way you are?

Discuss this story with your parents—how should you act if other children start teasing you?

THE STORY OF AWARENESS

There was once a group of children sitting together in a forest clearing, gathered to listen to a wise teacher known as the Buddha, who was visiting their village.

The Buddha picked up a beautiful red rose and held it before the children. He did not say anything and everyone was perfectly still. He held the flower in a most gentle, noble gesture, his thumb and forefinger holding the stem in such a way that it followed the shape of his hand. He held the rose in this way for a long time, still without saying anything. Everyone wondered what the teacher meant by this gesture.

Finally the Buddha looked up at the children and smiled. 'Children,' he said, 'this rose is a wondrous and beautiful thing. As I hold it you have a chance to experience it. You have a chance to make contact with a wondrous reality, to make contact with life itself.'

'You may say to yourself, "Why is he holding up this rose? What is the meaning of this?" However, if your mind is occupied by such thoughts, you cannot truly experience the flower. In the same way, being lost in thoughts is one of the things that prevents us from making true contact with life. If you are taken over by frustration, anxiety, worry or jealousy, you will lose the chance to make real contact with all the wonders of life.'

'There are people who can pass through a forest without ever really seeing one tree. In the same way, although life is filled with suffering, it also contains many wonders, which many people do not see.'

'So be aware, so you can see both the suffering and the wonders in life. Then you can be in touch with life and experience it deeply. You will then understand life, and this understanding will lead to love for everything that we are a part of.'

The children were deeply touched by the teacher's words, and each of them vowed to live a life of awareness. They promised to appreciate the wonders of life they encountered every day, like the beautiful rose.

When was the last time you noticed a beautiful flower, or anything else that reminded you of the wonder of life?

Try to notice when you are lost in thoughts such as worry or frustration. See if you can make true contact with life instead and notice how this can change the way you feel.

THE STORY OF APPRECIATION

High atop the snowy mountains between India, Nepal and China lies a country known as Tibet. In the middle east of this country is a small village called Happy Valley. The people in the village have no electricity, no cars or buses, no telephones, no television and no toys. They don't even have houses. Instead they live in tents which they make from yak hair.

In this village lives a family of four. The father's name is Yeshe and the mother's name is Tara. They have two children, one boy called Yori, who is six years old, and a girl called Chimey, who is four.

Each morning, Yori gets up at six o'clock, has breakfast and spends the rest of the day herding two hundred yaks over the mountains. The yaks run everywhere, so he is constantly running after them, trying to keep them together. He hardly gets a chance to rest for the whole day. Yori doesn't get to eat again until he returns home for dinner. He is so appreciative of his dinner each evening, and grateful to his mother for cooking it.

His sister Chimey gets up at seven o'clock, has breakfast and has to walk a very long way to the river to collect water, as the river is the closest source of water that isn't frozen over. As she is only small, Chimey can only carry a small amount at a time, so all day she has to walk back and forth from their tent to the river until they have enough water. The ground is very slippery because it is covered with snow, and Yori and Chimey are very cold because the temperature is sometimes minus thirty degrees.

Still Yori and Chimey appreciate the food they eat and the love of their family, and because of this they are very happy. They grow up to be very content and to care for each other and their family and friends. They are poor and yet they lead happy and healthy lives because they have learned to work for each other and not just for themselves.

There is another family who lives far away from Tibet, in a rich part of Melbourne by the sea. There are two children in this family, a boy named Peter, who is three years old, and a girl named Carly, who is five. They each have their own bedroom with a television, computer and many books and toys to play with. They get many wonderful presents at Christmas time and on their birthdays, and every year the family goes on an overseas holiday, to countries like England, Italy and Greece.

As the children get older they don't go to the beach as much as they used to. Instead they stay in their rooms watching movies or chatting on the internet. Peter asks the neighbour's children to play with him in the garden, but they tell him to leave them alone. Peter soon learns to amuse himself by playing computer games all on his own. Their Dad becomes busier and busier at work and doesn't get home till very late, while Mum is often away attending meetings.

Over time the family grows apart and doesn't spend much time together. They all have their own way of entertaining themselves and don't need each other's company. Peter becomes very quiet and doesn't talk much because he has become so accustomed to spending time alone playing computer games. Carly spends most of her time ringing boys and going out late at night, walking around the streets with her friends and sometimes getting drunk. As Mum is so busy working on different committees, she doesn't notice what is happening to her family, so she just makes sure they have plenty of new clothes and money for going out.

On the surface, this family may appear to have everything—all the material things that are meant to make us happy. However, over time they became distant, lonely and isolated. They lost sight of all their many blessings and failed to see the importance of caring for each other, leaving them unable to experience true happiness.

How do you think the Melbourne family might have acted differently if they had been more aware of their blessings?

How can you become more aware of your blessings?

How could you remind yourself to be grateful for what you have and to make the most of this?

At the end of each day you could try keeping a journal of all the things you are grateful for. Maybe you could ask your Mum and Dad to help you with this.

THE STORY OF COMPASSION

There was once a family of four, consisting of a mother, father, son and daughter. The boy's name was Adam and the girl was called Anne. Unfortunately, their father was an alcoholic and their mother was a drug addict. Because of the parents' addictions they were very poor, and often they couldn't even afford the basics for living, such as food and clothing.

As they didn't own a car and had no money for any other means of transport, the children went to the only school that was within walking distance of their home. The school was not a very good one. The teachers were not very attentive, the buildings were run-down and the classes were overcrowded. It was difficult for the children to learn.

Sometimes the family didn't have any food at all—the pantry was completely bare. On these occasions Adam and Anne would go together to the local church to get food. They became good friends with the priest at the church who was very kind and compassionate. Whenever they were together, he taught them about kindness and compassion, and the children put his advice into practice in their everyday lives.

'Practising compassion gives you more inner strength and calm,' he would tell them. 'You will be able to help others, but even if you can't it doesn't matter, because you will be the real winner. Through acting compassionately you benefit 100% of the time.'

After much thought, Adam and Anne realised that this must be true. They tried to practise compassion wherever they went and towards whoever they were with—even people they did not like. They always put others before themselves. They would try to imagine how they would feel if they were in the shoes of other people. Every day they put this into practice, and they soon found they had forgotten about their own problems because they were always thinking of others. As a consequence, they developed greater inner strength and were never miserable about their situation.

This practice of compassion began at home. Their parents often argued, and their Mum was depressed a lot of the time. Adam and Anne both tried to tell her that things would get better and that she was not a terrible mother. Though their Dad got angry with them at times, they also tried to not hold this against him. He had a lot of stress and worries in his life, and though his actions were bad, they knew he was a good person who deep down just wanted himself and his family to be happy.

Adam and Anne became very well known and respected in their community. With their help, their parents managed to overcome their addictions. They had then gone on to help friends of their parents who had similar problems. They often visited the elderly and the sick and were always kind to their neighbours. One day a TV reporter heard about Adam and Anne and decided to broadcast a story on the 'compassionate kids'.

As a result of the TV exposure, a lot of money was raised by the community to enable Adam and Anne to get a good education. They went to a great school and then onto university, both achieving very good grades. Once they had completed their education, they returned to their community and became great teachers. They taught others everything they had learnt themselves; that we can change anything for the better as long as we practise compassion. We can change how we get on with our parents, our friends, as well as total strangers, and we can even change the world in some small way.

Would you like to live a life of compassion like Adam and Anne?

What would you be missing out on if you always thought of others before yourself? What would you gain?

How could you start acting compassionately in your life today?

A SPECIAL STORY FOR OLDER CHILDREN— THE STORY OF INNER FREEDOM

In T'ien-chu city there were two Chinese boys who studied at the same school and were good friends. One was called Fuzu and the other's name was Jujan. Both of their fathers had been killed by Chinese government soldiers. Both boys were weighed down by a heavy sadness in their hearts.

They asked many adults why it was that their fathers had been killed. The adults told them, 'Unfortunately, we have no human rights and no real freedom in this country.'

Many times they asked the adults, 'How do we achieve freedom?' Some said they could never attain freedom, believing the people would forever be under the control of the government and that they simply had to accept this. Others told them that if they learned the law then maybe they could find some freedom.

So both boys decided to study law after they graduated from high school, as they wanted to find an answer to their question. However, they soon realised that although in theory the law was just and fair, what was written down was not always practised. Sadly, many government officials and police were corrupt. If someone reported a crime, it was often not followed up because someone else paid a bribe to stop the report. The two boys then realised that understanding the law didn't really help all that much—it helped more to have money. They therefore stopped studying the law because they thought it was pointless.

One day the two boys arranged a meeting with a retired politician who had a very good knowledge of international law and politics. They asked him the same question, 'How can we attain freedom?'

He replied, 'If you want individual freedom, you have to emigrate to a democratic country such as Switzerland or the United States. However, if you want inner freedom, you have to ask a very experienced and wise monk; he will tell you.'

Fuzu didn't understand what the politician meant by 'inner freedom', although he understood very well what individual freedom meant. He said to Jujan, 'I want to move to Shanghai and then try to get to America. Will you come with me?'

Jujan replied, 'Before we seek individual freedom in a western country, perhaps we should first discover what inner freedom is.'

Fuzu didn't agree, so he went to Shanghai by himself and then arranged a tourist visa for America. Once in America, he was able to obtain a refugee visa.

At first Fuzu thought his new life in America was fantastic. He was very happy with the political system and the many opportunities there were for him to live the life he wanted. He found a good job and married an American woman, with whom he had four children. He wanted many children because in China you were only allowed one child.

However, despite their individual freedoms, Fuzu and his wife were not content with what they had. This discontentment eventually caused a breakdown in their marriage, finally ending in divorce. Fuzu remarried twice after this, but things only got worse and not better. He had many children with the different women he married but was rarely able to spend time with them because they were busy with their own lives. His life turned out to be very stressful and lonely. Eventually he turned to alcohol and drugs to help him cope with his situation. Both his mental and physical health became increasingly worse because of this.

Meanwhile, Jujan arranged a meeting with a Chinese monk and asked him how he could attain inner freedom.

The monk replied, 'I can't give you an instant answer, but if you become a monk perhaps you will find out for yourself what inner freedom means. There is a Tibetan monastery called *Zamthang* in Shechuan province which you may like to go to. I visited this monastery a few years ago and was very impressed. The only problem, however, is they do not speak Chinese, only Tibetan.'

Jujan thanked the monk for his advice. He felt so inspired when he heard the name of this monastery that he set off immediately, journeying there by bus and then truck. When he arrived and met the abbot, Lama Lobsang, he was incredibly moved. When he looked into the lama's eyes, he could tell that he knew the secret to a deeper inner freedom than he had ever imagined. Soon Jujan told the lama he wished to dedicate his life to attaining inner freedom.

The lama replied, 'Are you sure? There is no guarantee how long it will take; but if this is your wish, you have to study the Tibetan language and Buddhist practice.'

Jujan was determined. He was ordained as a Buddhist monk and diligently studied the Tibetan language and also studied Buddhism with the help of a translator. After three years of study he was able to read and communicate fluently in Tibetan. He then devoted eight years to Buddhist study, practice and meditation He became a fine example of a Buddhist monk.

One day the Chinese authorities visited Jujan's monastery, as they did all the Tibetan monasteries, and ordered all the monks to sign a form. The form was written in Chinese, so the monks had no idea what they were signing; they were just told it was an agreement against 'enemies of our country'.

Jujan read the form and was very upset to discover the Chinese were hiding the true intention and meaning contained in the form. It was in fact a declaration that the monks were against the Dalai Lama, the Buddhist spiritual leader. Jujan refused to sign the form and told the other monks to refuse as well. He then got into a fight with one of the Chinese officials. They tried to arrest Jujan but he put up a brave fight, and some of the other monks even tried to help him. After struggling like this for a few minutes he managed to break away from the authorities and escape, thinking this was his best option. After this incident he knew it was not safe to return to the monastery, so he decided to gather his belongings and join a small group of Tibetans who were trekking across the Himalayan Mountains, hoping to escape to India.

The escapees had to take a long route to avoid the Chinese soldiers, and the trip ended up taking one and a half months. Many were injured along the way, as the tracks were very rough and slippery, covered with ice, snow and sometimes dense, thorny scrub. During the trek, Jujan fell in love with a Tibetan girl in the group, Pema. As she had been to a Chinese school, she could speak Chinese fluently. They began talking to each other and soon found they had many things in common.

After many adventures they arrived at the Tibetan refugee reception in Nepal, and later travelled onwards to India. When they finally arrived they had to enrol in an adult boarding school, where over a thousand adult Tibetan refugees were fed, sheltered and educated free. Only a small number of the students were women because it was generally easier for men to travel long distances and women were therefore scarce.

One day a man with a great deal of money and status fell in love with Jujan's girlfriend and the couple separated. Jujan's heart was completely broken. He could not study or sleep at all. He left the school but he had nowhere to live and no food, so he went to a monastery and begged for food, sleeping in the forest for a few weeks. Soon he decided he couldn't keep living like this.

He thought to himself, 'I have been through so much heartbreak and suffering. I really don't care all that much about money, girlfriends or what other people think of me. Now I see the truth that these things are not the true source of happiness, I just want to live a simple life and go back to my original goal. What I want most of all is to find inner freedom.'

He went to the Dalai Lama's office and they agreed to give him regular money for food and other basic needs if he practised genuinely. They offered him one of the retreat huts high in the mountain forest to live in. He stayed there for fifteen years, completely focusing his mind and discovering the peaceful natural state of mind which is free from the control of thoughts and emotions.

Most people have uncontrolled emotions, so if, for example, someone is unfortunate enough to have some property stolen, become ill or have to end a close relationship, they will normally be very sad or depressed. Controlled as they are by their emotions, they will react like this, but Jujan overcame the control his emotions had over him. He completely recovered from his heartbreak and was no longer a slave to the whims of his emotions. He could live off only very little food for sustenance and be completely happy all by himself. He could even cure all his own illnesses without the help of a doctor. When he heard his family had died he was not upset; he realised death is an inevitable part of life and accepted this with compassion and humility. Jujan's story spread throughout India and he became quite famous. He didn't allow visitors to come but many reporters and tourists took his photo from a distance.

One day he received a letter from a big Chinese temple in America, asking him to visit and bless their temple, as well as conduct some teachings. He accepted the invitation because he had a vision that he would meet his old friend Fuzu, and he was pleased to be able to speak about his experiences for the first time in his native language.

When he arrived in America and entered the temple he performed a few ceremonies to bless the area and gave some teachings. Many people came to hear him. At that time Fuzu was undergoing great mental suffering, so he was searching for spiritual comfort. For this reason he came to the temple. He had no idea that his old friend Jujan would be there, and was amazed when he saw him. Jujan let Fuzu stay with him overnight in the temple. For the entire night they talked about how Fuzu had found individual freedom, while Jujan had discovered inner freedom.

What do you need in order to achieve individual freedom? What do you need to find inner freedom?

Which do you think is the most valuable form of freedom?

How can we learn to be in control of our happiness?

How could you find inner freedom in your life without going to a monastery or leaving your current situation?

Reread all these stories many times over to understand more about their hidden meanings. Learn about the qualities of happiness now and try your best to practise them all the time, so that you can lead a truly happy life.

Setting Out in the Right Direction

I feel very strongly about teaching important messages to teenagers, because this is such a crucial time in one's life and we only have one chance to get it right. If we miss this opportunity we will never have another chance. Therefore if you have a teenage son or daughter I hope you can encourage them to read this chapter. If you are in this age group yourself, I urge you to reflect upon this chapter carefully.

As a teenager we are young, smart and energetic, so we can make decisions that will lead us to having great life experiences, to the development of great wisdom and towards making a big impact on the world. On the other hand, because we are inexperienced we may be lacking in wisdom, and this means we can make decisions which will damage or reduce our potential and cause ourselves or those around us great suffering.

It is commonly believed that teenagers never listen to advice given by older people because they are too distracted, too proud or have no appreciation for the opinions of older generations. I do not believe this is necessarily true, however I have observed that young people sometimes do feel proud of what they have so far learned and experienced in their relatively short lives and therefore feel reluctant to accept that there is still much more to learn. This can be a sign that they lack wisdom, as the wiser we are, the more we should want to learn from others.

It is my profound wish that you will read this chapter and analyse what it has to say. After all, regardless of whether you are a teenager or not, there is no doubt that, like everybody else, you are seeking to achieve happiness and avoid suffering in your life.

HOW TO DEVELOP FOCUS

As I have mentioned earlier, the root causes of happiness remain the same whether we are one year old or a hundred years old, but as a teenager we have special challenges to face and special decisions to make. We therefore need to place an emphasis on some specific qualities.

Many people have great regret when, having reached adulthood, they look back at their teenage years. They dwell on all the time and energy they wasted and yearn to become a teenager again to experience it differently, however, it is not possible to turn back time. It is therefore incredibly important to be aware of the special opportunities the teenage years give us and to use them wisely.

It sometimes seems odd that teenagers, who because of their youth naturally have so much energy and intelligence, tend to waste this so much more than older people. What causes teenagers to behave like this? I believe it is because we often lack an inner focus at this age and therefore get easily distracted by everything going on around us. We become absorbed by the products of popular culture, such as movies and the internet. We have a body that is undergoing quite a radical transformation and that new thing called 'romantic love' seems to consume much of our time and energy.

It is natural that we want to be liked by our peer group and we experiment with many new things, yet we are just starting out on life's journey and therefore may be emotionally immature. Short-term relationships can be a feature of this time because we get bored very easily or have unrealistic expectations. Boredom is common because we are so reliant on external stimulation—if we don't get enough stimulation we are likely to lose interest, as our need for external things to satisfy us is stronger than our drive to learn.

It is strange that we are so taken up by external concerns when our view of the world and the scope of our knowledge are so limited! This doesn't mean that we are stupid. It does mean, however, that because of our relative lack of life experience we find it hard to know what is important to focus on and what is not. Until we have developed a mature enough view, we will scatter our energy on whatever happens to appear in front of us. Furthermore, our minds may be so overcome with emotions that we often don't care about the consequences of our actions because we don't really realise what they are. The most important thing for you as a teenager is therefore to carefully consider the motivation behind your actions as well as their consequences.

Exercise: Here is a simple exercise aimed at helping you plan for the future and improving your focus. Every day, maybe early in the morning or last thing before you go to bed, spend five minutes thinking about what you have done that day. Spend this time reflecting on the decisions you have made and the actions you have taken. For example, did anything upset you or make you angry? How did you deal with the emotions you felt? How did they influence your actions and decisions? Think carefully about the likely short-term and long-term consequences of your actions. Think about all your decisions and all your actions, no matter how small or big they seem. This will help with your long-term mental focus and ability to plan for your future.

WHAT DO I WANT TO DO WITH MY LIFE?

As teenagers we are like a new bud starting to open in the spring. We have the beauty and freshness of youth and the possibility of a full and rich life ahead of us. All the wonderful possibilities of life are ours. We can be rich and famous, a world leader or a hero. We can help reduce global warming, cure life-debilitating diseases or prevent starvation. We have all these possibilities at our fingertips—anything is possible! And yet it seems so difficult to know what to do. How do we know which path to take? Who do we choose as our role models? What do we do to get where we want to go? What are the ultimate advantages when we do get there? What we are ultimately looking for is our own identity, which is of course a very significant thing to be searching for.

Because we are so easily distracted we often tend to find something convenient and unchallenging to engage and distract our minds. Often we spend endless hours chatting on the internet, sending text messages or listening to music. Our minds become trained to behave in this way, always looking outwards for pleasure and distraction rather than inwards. We find it very difficult to just be with ourselves or to think about plans for our future. Even when we try to picture the future and the possibilities open to us, it is easy to become immersed in fantasy or to just follow what our friends are doing.

So here is some practical advice to consider when you deliberate your future:

1. Do you have the necessary attributes to achieve your chosen goal?

If you wish to be a famous singer or a well-known actor, you're likely to need good looks, a melodious voice and the ability to work very hard as well as good fortune! You must ask yourself: Do I *really* possess all these attributes? Do I have the confidence and determination to pursue this goal? Am I sure I won't give up half way because it's too difficult? Do I have the diligence and perseverance to achieve my goals? Am I pursuing this goal because I really want to and not because someone else expects it of me?[17]

If your answer is 'yes' to these five questions, then you can go for it! You have what it takes and are very likely to be successful. If, however, you are not sure about any of these questions, then this type of goal is unlikely to be worth pursuing and you may just be pursuing a fantasy and wasting your energy. If all your precious time and energy is being wasted, this stops you from achieving something else.

2. Will this goal benefit you for all of your life?

If you are quite sure and determined to achieve a specific goal and this goal is realistic, then it is likely you will achieve it, however, you still have to carefully contemplate whether this goal will benefit you and still be meaningful many years later.

If your goal is to become a famous singer or sports star, for example, you should carefully consider the consequences of putting all your energy into realising such a dream. First you need to consider that only a very few exceptional people can make a living with this kind of career, and you may be condemning yourself to a life of great financial hardship. Furthermore, it can be very hard to settle down if you constantly need to move location in order to find work, and then if you are successful, when you become older there may no longer be any demand for your skills. You may then have difficulty leading a normal life, especially if you have been living in a make-believe world or have never experienced much hardship.

It may sound a bit strange but in Tibet some of the monks and nuns are the famous people, just like movie stars in western culture. Personally, I never wanted to become a popular lama in Tibet because I would always have had to act in a certain way and be extremely conscious of my conduct. I would have been always surrounded by many people and unable to relax and live naturally.

Have you really thought about how pursuing and achieving your goal will affect your life? Are you still determined to achieve this goal, and do you think it would give you a meaningful life? Are there better ways to pursue a meaningful life? If you are self-conscious and would find a life of fame disturbing, then you are wasting your precious time and energy fantasising about it. Recognise this and start to look at the innumerable other possibilities, analysing each of these options carefully, then when you have chosen the goal that is right for you, focus with single-minded determination on achieving it. If you try to second-guess or doubt yourself then you can become confused and lose your path.

If you find it too difficult to completely dedicate your life to something without any doubt, then you need to plan to achieve what you want in stages. Though it is good to be confident that you will be able to achieve your ideal goals, it is always best to anticipate challenges and have a backup plan. If your highest goal doesn't work out, you should not be disheartened because your plan should include many different levels of achievement, including the worst case scenario. You should have the highest aspirations but also be prepared to be satisfied with the worst result. But never stop trying to achieve!

It is easy to think that if we work hard then our life will be harder. We must always remind ourselves, however, that the opposite can be true, as our life can actually become easier in the long run, and we can even reach a stage where what once seemed like hard work becomes effortless. On the other hand, if we are lazy or complacent our life may look easy but in fact it will turn out to be much more difficult. One word of caution, though. For some people there is a danger of being too goal-focused and then neglecting family, friends and other important aspects of life, but for most of us, putting a lot of energy into our principal goal is a very worthwhile and valuable pursuit, as long as we do not forget these other dimensions of life.

The discipline of consistent hard work can also improve our ability to focus and concentrate. By working hard at something we consider worthwhile, we can become more efficient and clearer in our thinking, and eventually we can experience an innate sense of joy and satisfaction while absorbed in a particular task. When we become more efficient we find it easier to provide for our material needs, and we can then choose to use this as a basis for simplifying our lives and devoting our time to other important pursuits, such as cultivating friendships, developing new interests and skills, or even choosing to lead a spiritual life. More will be said about this in the following chapters.

Before I proceed, here is a short story that illustrates the importance of determination. It is my hope that you will understand why the lives of the two main characters turned out so differently, and appreciate the impact of the choices they made when they were young.

A TALE OF DETERMINATION

There are two boys who study together in the Tibetan Children's Village (TCV) in Dharamsala, northern India, which is like a boarding school for young Tibetan children. Tenzin was born in Dharamsala and grew up there, while the other boy, Jigme, was born in Golok, a province in Tibet. The two boys are very competitive and are always competing against each other in their studies.

Tibetans and many Asian people believe that western countries provide far greater opportunities, especially when it comes to work and study. When Tenzin grows up, his father, who is a Tibetan government official, will be able to send him to Switzerland to have a better education and a better life. Tenzin tells Jigme about this, boasting that he will have a much more successful future than his schoolmate.

Though Jigme is upset that he won't have the opportunities granted to Tenzin, he promises himself he will study very hard to catch up with his friend.

When Tenzin arrives in Switzerland, he feels like he is in heaven and simply can't believe how fortunate he is. Everything is so beautiful and all his needs are easily met. When he goes to school, he has no problem with language because he studied English in India. He thinks to himself, 'I have to study very hard and get a good education so I can work for the welfare of the Tibetan people in the future.'

However, after a few weeks of diligent study, many distractions cause him to lose his focus. As Tenzin does not have such a strong character, he becomes preoccupied with other things and loses his determination to study. Often when people are faced with many distractions and opportunities to have fun, they begin wanting more and more things and lose sight of their original goals, as they are so focused on present pleasure. Eventually, unable to find a job after completing his studies, Tenzin becomes depressed. He starts to drink heavily in order to help himself cope. His life becomes much worse than when he was living in Dharamsala.

For Jigme, moving to a western country is out of the question, as it is impossible for him to obtain a visa and he has very little money. He continues to study very hard in the Tibetan Children's Village school, but after he graduates he cannot enrol in further education because he would have to go to an Indian school and pay fees.

So Jigme rents a very basic kitchen, where he both sleeps and lives, supporting himself by making and selling food. Every day he gets up at four o'clock in the morning and for two hours makes bread, which he then sells on the street. He comes home to study advanced English, mathematics and computer science, which he does by correspondence. From four until six in the evening he cooks momos, which are similar to dim sims but a more rounded shape, with vegetables or meat inside. He sells them every evening and then continues to study until midnight. He has no fun activities or pleasures to distract him. Occasionally he feels sad and lonely but he never has any time to dwell on this! For over five years he lives in this way, continuing his incredibly hard work.

One day Jigme meets a grey-haired western woman called Isobel, who asks him a few questions while he is selling momos. They get on really well with each other, and before long she invites him out to dinner. It turns out Isobel is from Switzerland, though she visits Dharamsala regularly because she is helping several Tibetan politicians in her home country. When she asks Jigme what his goal is, he tells her that he wishes to go to university and become a professor.

After dinner, Jigme takes Isobel to see where he lives. Shocked by his poor situation and moved by his determination, she offers to sponsor him to attend university in Switzerland. Jigme is speechless.

For some time Jigme thinks this is all a dream, and he worries a great deal that Isobel will change her mind. But before he knows what has happened, Isobel goes to Delhi and arranges a visa for him. He simply can't believe that he is fortunate enough to go to Switzerland!

Before Jigme sets off he catches up with his best friend, a young monk called Konchok, who congratulates him but then says in a more serious tone of voice, 'You have to remember two things when you are in Switzerland. First, it is human nature that when you have more and are living in better conditions, it is easy to lose focus and discipline. If you don't lose your focus you can achieve many things and live a happy life, but if you fall prey to greed or laziness you will encounter great suffering. Secondly, you should never forget the welfare of the Tibetan people, no matter how good your situation is.'

Jigme promises Konchok he will never forget these things.

A week later, Jigme gets the visa and moves to Switzerland. When he arrives he is amazed, thinking he is in heaven just like Tenzin. The only difference is that every day Jigme keeps in his mind the advice of his best friend. He studies psychology with great effort at university for seven years, and also works as a graphic designer using his computer skills. After a year of living in Switzerland, he falls in love with Isobel's daughter, Heidi, and after several years they marry. Two years later he becomes a professor in psychology and opens up his own practice, which is extremely successful.

One day Professor Jigme gives a public lecture at a famous university in Zurich. By this time Tenzin is still unemployed, lonely and has started taking drugs. He comes to the lecture because it is about psychology and therefore might help him. When he arrives he thinks the lecturer looks very familiar. In the middle of the lecture, Jigme recounts going to school at the Tibetan Children's Village and having a classmate called Tenzin. He mentions that he moved to Switzerland about fourteen years ago but never heard what happened to him. Tenzin is shocked, realising this is his classmate Jigme who is giving the lecture. He cannot believe that his old rival had become so successful while his life has turned out to be such a failure.

Think about how it is that two boys with such a similar background could grow up so differently. Do you remember the two things that were most important for Jigme, inspiring him to achieve what he did? Also think about how you could inspire your life with a goal that is truly meaningful for you and what a difference this could make.

THE NECESSITY OF SELF-CONFIDENCE

As teenagers we are acutely sensitive to the opinions of others. Again, this is because we have not yet developed enough inner focus to know ourselves and to really appreciate the positive and negative consequences of our actions. One who has much experience and wisdom will never be self-conscious. This is because they can judge for themselves what is good and what is bad, what is worthwhile and what is not, what to concentrate their energy upon and what is a waste of time. As teenagers, however, our relatively limited worldly experience means we are unlikely to have this kind of discriminating awareness. Our perception is narrow, like the eye of a needle, and we can easily fall into the trap of relying too much on the opinions of others.

This is not only true for teenagers in the West. Even in my small village in Tibet I was obsessed with my image and was very self-conscious about what other people thought. I always acted naturally with my family and relatives, as I didn't feel it was so important for things to be perfect with them. However, if my friends or others from the community came to our house, whatever I did and however my parents, brother and sisters and even my relatives behaved, I would be utterly embarrassed unless it was all perfect. When I look back now, it is clear to me that I was acting falsely in front of my friends and acquaintances, just because I was desperate for them to have a good opinion of me.

As teenagers our circle of influence is generally limited. As a result, our understanding of just what is possible is also limited. We want lots of friends, we want to be liked and we want to be popular, so we tend to follow the interests of those in our peer group. We try to be funny and entertaining. Boys, particularly, want their peer group to see them as 'cool', and to maintain this image they might boast about their girl-friends or make fun of others. Girls, on the other hand, tend to worry about their looks and spend a great deal of time and money on make-up, clothes and haircuts so they feel more attractive. Image is the most important focus, and this emphasis is encouraged by the media and our peer group.

However, if we reflect carefully, we will find that we are only concerned about how people our own age perceive us, without really caring what the rest of the world thinks of us. Nor are we really concerned about the future consequences of being so concerned about our good self-image. If this becomes an obsession, we may become blind to the many things which are truly valuable in the world. Sometimes we decorate our beautiful young bodies with tattoos or piercing. Although there is nothing wrong with wanting to look beautiful and be proud of your unique identity, try to remember that one day you may be embarrassed to see the excessive ways in which you have adorned your body for the sake of self-image. Just remember, fashion changes very quickly!

Sometimes an obsession with self-image can lead us into even more damaging behaviour. We are all aware of the harmful effects of drugs, cigarettes and alcohol, yet we are often enticed into trying them to appear 'cool' in front of our peers or to compensate for a lack of self-confidence. Knowing this, we need the determination, self-discipline and wisdom to safeguard our physical and mental health from the effects of these harmful substances.

As we become older and more experienced, most people gain in self-confidence and stop worrying so much about what others think, no longer being driven by the desire to be popular. We also acquire the wisdom to make better decisions, based on our own observations rather than the opinions of others. Unfortunately, there is no magical trick to suddenly give us inner focus and self-knowledge, as we need to achieve this for ourselves as we learn and grow with life experience. However, whenever you find yourself trying to impress another person, it is helpful to ask yourself this question: Why is their opinion so important to me? And what do I *myself* think about this matter? Constantly reflecting in this way will help us to develop inner focus, and we will gradually come to understand our own mind.

SEX, DRUGS AND ROCK AND ROLL

Earlier I mentioned some of the self-harming behaviours that people experiment with when they are teenagers, especially drugs and excessive alcohol consumption. I am very much against drug and alcohol use, perhaps because I was never exposed to them when growing up and can therefore easily see the harm they can cause. In the West, men often feel pressured to drink alcohol to appear more masculine or 'manly', and some women seem to think that drinking will make them more outgoing, confident and desirable to men. These ideas are often promoted by a society with a limited or narrow view and a lack of alternative cultural influences. For example, in the Golok province of Tibet, none of the women smoke or drink, and only about five percent of men partake in these activities.

Many people believe that a life without alcohol or drugs is a boring life, but I would question this idea. Do you think somebody who has never had a headache is more boring than a person who has a headache and relieves it with medication? Similarly, is someone with no itch more boring than someone who has an itch but scratches and relieves it? We can think of intoxicants as an example of what Buddhists mean by becoming addicted to a craving—using a drug gives us a pleasurable sensation and this leads to a craving for more of that sensation. Eventually, there may come a point when the craving has taken over our lives and we spend all of our time just trying to fulfill that craving, without ever truly satisfying it. I am not saying that drugs are not enjoyable or fun when you take them; rather, there can be an extremely unpleasant effect when the drug wears off, you can do some very harmful things while under the influence of these drugs, and there is a great danger that you will lose control over your life.

Even if we do not become addicted, taking drugs can seriously damage the body and the mind. Just taking drugs once can trigger a serious mental illness or can cause us to engage in damaging behaviours. I have often heard stories from my doctor friends of young people they have seen in hospital emergency departments who have taken drugs and hurt themselves or others while under the influence of these drugs. All drugs can do this. Even drugs that you may think are harmless, like marijuana, can have detrimental effects on the brain and lead to serious mental illnesses like schizophrenia.

Unfortunately, many young people have the idea that drugs lead to spiritual experiences, mistaking seeing or feeling unusual things as 'spiritual progress'. This is a completely distorted view, because spiritual realisation should make us become more self-controlled, more grounded and more in touch with reality. In contrast, drugs make us lose self-control, lead to experiences which are purely illusory and make us lose touch with reality.

In the same way that a craving for the sensations generated by drugs can be overpowering, so too can a craving for the sensation of sexual pleasure. Many people in the West seem to think that the desire for sex or falling in love is an unstoppable and overpowering force of nature, and many also seem to think that, unlike drugs or alcohol, sex is a natural desire or even a necessity in life. Of course it is true that no human being would exist without the sexual union of their parents, and I am not saying that sex is necessarily bad or unwholesome. However, there are two important points which I think we should consider.

The first is that our motivation for sexual activity is very important. Are we thinking about sex with a pure intention, to show our genuine love and caring for someone or to have children to carry wisdom to the next generation? Or do we want to have sex to satisfy an unrealistic expectation or fantasy, due to loss of self-control, or even because we want to look good in front of our peers? It is important to understand that the sexual energy between a man and a woman has incredible potential to develop into something much deeper and more powerful than most people are aware of, even an extraordinary inner capacity. However, in order to discover this, many conditions must be present in each person; in particular, both partners must have pure intentions and the relationship can never be forced—it must always form naturally.

If you cannot relate to this idea, it is important to at least know that sexual relationships are not nearly as simple as we may think. In fact, it is possible to identify eight different levels of complexity, progressively more deep and meaningful.

The lowest is the animal level, which is when we are just looking for a physical sensation or to satisfy an urge or appetite, such as we do when we eat and drink.

The second level is the transaction level, at which we have a little more understanding of what we are doing, but the motivation is based on greed, so there is very little chance to develop any real connection. Casual relationships often occur at this level.

The third level is that of ordinary human sexuality. This is where sexual union takes place between two people who have fallen in love, so there is a greater sense of connection, more enjoyment and a better relationship. However, this type of attraction is usually based on blind attachment and is unlikely to meet anything more than short-term physical and emotional needs.

The fourth level is the educated level, at which the needs of both partners are better met because they possess greater knowledge. They have a greater ability to deal with problems and improve their relationship, though the depth of their relationship is limited because this knowledge occurs mainly at an intellectual level. The love between the two partners is still a little fabricated, not nearly as natural or spontaneous as it could be.

Next we have the fifth level—the level of good conditions—where the physical wellbeing and emotional maturity of both partners are more developed and there is a natural outflow of generosity and appreciation. This gives true love more of a chance to blossom, and the level of sexual gratification is also much higher.

The sixth level is that of spiritual emergence. At this stage, all of the good inner qualities we have mentioned in this book are highly developed in both partners, especially generosity, gratitude and pure perception. Our experience of bliss is more profound, not only on the level of sensation but at a level beyond conventional thought, and this bliss contains a form of innate, natural wisdom.

The seventh level is the spiritual mastery level. All previous qualities are developed, as well as the power to control the flow of energy in what we call the 'subtle body',[18] made up of channels, inner wind and subtle essences. The subtle body is not something that exists objectively; rather it describes the blissful currents of energy which are experienced while embraced in sexual union. The union of wisdom and blissful awareness becomes greater and greater, with or without a partner, until it becomes totally independent of external conditions.

Finally, the eighth level is totally beyond concepts such as space and time, and can be thought of as the inseparable union of wisdom and immutable blissful awareness, or enlightenment itself.

Even if this doesn't make sense to us, just having some curiosity and an aspiration to find out more about these higher levels puts us at a great advantage. Basically, the crucial point is to try to develop an attitude of genuine generosity and appreciation. Developing a better or purer perception of our partner is much more important than looking for perfection in them, as how we see them depends mostly on the way we think—as Shakespeare said, 'Nothing is good or bad but thinking makes it so'. It is important to at least aspire towards thinking of sex as something rare and precious; if we think it is just a basic need that you routinely require, like food or drink, we will never go beyond the lower stages and will be at a great disadvantage.

The second point I would like to make is that sex is not a necessity in life for everyone. A rich, fulfilling life with many accomplishments can be achieved without sex—in fact, this can sometimes be achieved much easier without sex! What I mean here is that many difficulties can arise as a result of sexuality, including situations which lead to jealousy, anger, regret or obsessions with one or more people. These all take us away from focusing on what is truly important in our lives. This does not mean we should not love others or should avoid intimate relationships; rather, we should realise that fulfilling relationships can be built without sex, and these often contain far fewer self-centred concerns than relationships where sex is of primary importance.

HOW TO HAVE BETTER RELATIONSHIPS

Before you criticise someone you should walk a mile in their shoes. —Traditional saying.—

～

Teenagers often think the concept of a 'relationship' refers primarily to a boyfriend-girlfriend relationship. However, the most important relationships we have as a teenager are those with our family and friends. Relationships are of supreme importance throughout our lives. When they are going well we feel better within ourselves, surrounded by those who love and care for us. When they are going badly they can make us feel terrible. Many people believe that whether we get along with somebody or not is totally out of our control, as though it is a kind of instinct. However, the truth is that we all have a great deal of control over the quality of our relationships, and it is helpful to know how we can use this to our advantage, especially to overcome conflict.

When I was young I became dissatisfied with my home and often went to great lengths to get my father's permission to stay at our neighbour's place. Regardless of how nice my home was or how delicious the food was, I looked elsewhere to homes that were sometimes uncomfortable, even dirty, with the food bland and basic.

As teenagers, many of us start to find life with our families dull and boring, so we seek freedom and independence elsewhere. However, because we lack the ability to support ourselves financially, and therefore cannot move out of home, it is hard for us to be truly independent. So we enter into different circles of friends and want to spend more time with them than with our family—and this may cause conflict at home.

There are of course many, many other things which can cause conflict between teenagers and their parents—or for that matter between teenagers and anyone else! We may think our parents are boring and old-fashioned, or we might think they do not trust us enough and are making us look stupid in front of our friends. Yet no matter what we are arguing about or who we are arguing with, the methods to solve conflicts with others are always the same.

Every human being, no matter how different we are, has the same basic needs and the same basic wish to be happy. If we want to resolve conflicts with others we need to remember that we are like them so that we can understand why they are behaving in the way they are. Try to put yourself in the other person's position for a little while. If you have a conflict with your mother, try to imagine that you are in her situation. If you really try you will be able to get some idea of how she is feeling and why she is behaving in the way that she is. Think of how you would like to be treated if you were in her situation, even if you think she is wrong, and treat her in this way. Imagine you have children yourself and how you would like them to treat you, and then treat your parents in the same way.

Remember, we are not concerned about what is right or wrong, but rather with finding the most skilful way to deal with a particular situation. We can practise this same technique with any relationship in our life—for example, with our teachers, our siblings or our friends. The insight we can gain into why others behave as they do is truly amazing if we can put ourselves in their position.

GRATITUDE

Feeling gratitude towards others also improves our relationships with them; and as I have mentioned before, gratitude is one of the core mental qualities which lead to happiness. Here is a way you can generate gratitude towards your parents. Think about what your parents have done for you over the years—caring for your physical needs and teaching you the ways of the world—and think of all the effort and sacrifices they have made for you. Even if you have had a difficult relationship with them at times, there is no-one else who will have done as much for you. If you really think about this you cannot but feel a sense of gratitude! This feeling of gratitude can help us feel happy both directly and indirectly. It brings an immediate sense of warmth and closeness, and in the long-run our relationship is sure to improve as we will treat them with greater kindness.

If, however, we find it difficult to be grateful to our parents, remember they may be under the control of negative emotions, as we all can be at times. Rather than holding a critical or hostile attitude or becoming despondent, we can use this as an opportunity to increase our empathy towards them and develop greater emotional strength. If we respond to them with anger or by holding a grudge, we miss a precious opportunity to show that we really care deeply about them.

I am often surprised when I talk to young people in the West about feeling gratitude towards their parents. Generally, parents try to provide their children with every possible advantage, yet it is still commonplace for young people to complain about them and perhaps feel unloved. This is quite different from the environment I grew up in. Looking from the outside, Tibetan parents seem much stricter than western parents and will often use physical punishment if their children disobey them. However, in Tibetan culture, which is largely influenced by Buddhism, respect and gratitude towards one's parents are greatly emphasised and it is very rare to blame one's parents for life's difficulties. Although analysing our family situation can provide us with certain insights, it is never useful if it leads to blame and resentment.

THE IMPORTANCE OF COMPASSION

Maybe you are thinking, 'Well, I have a conflict with my sister or my mother, but this conflict is not my fault—it is her fault!' Perhaps you have tried really hard to understand why she is behaving in this way and have still come to the conclusion that she is completely to blame. I don't think this is the case very often by the way—most of the time when we have truly tried to appreciate another person's point of view, we find that we are also partially at fault, however, if we have genuinely tried to consider the other person's point of view and honestly feel we have done all that is possible to resolve the conflict, but still to no avail, maybe then we think we have a right to feel angry and hurt by the other person.

I ask you, though, by feeling anger and resentment, who are you hurting? Let me explain. Just say we have had a fight with our friend because they have become fond of another person. We feel jealous and hurt that they seem to be placing all their attention and spending all their time with this new friend while ignoring us. Maybe they aren't taking our feelings into consideration, being focused purely on themselves, and this is causing us to suffer. We could respond to this by dwelling on the bad qualities of our friend or thinking of how unfortunate we are, allowing anger and jealousy to eat away at us—yet this will only cause us to suffer. We are likely to dwell upon this situation more and more as the small flame of anger and jealousy turns into a raging wildfire, totally destroying our peace of mind. Alternatively, we could think, 'Well, this friend is making me suffer because of her own narrow way of thinking, which will actually cause her harm in the long term. Instead of being angry I will practise forgiveness and compassion.'

Try your hardest to evoke kind and loving thoughts towards this friend, thinking of all the things you like about her. When you feel kindness and compassion towards her, you will feel happiness growing inside you. I guarantee it.

A LITTLE BIT ABOUT FREEDOM

I mentioned earlier that, as teenagers, we often want autonomy or 'freedom'. In the modern world, however, many people seem to confuse false freedom with true or inner freedom. False freedom includes the freedom to do whatever we please, and also freedom from having to depend upon other people. This type of freedom creates a distance between ourselves and others. Ultimately it results in loneliness, as we come to accept and reject people according to our needs instead of relating to them through genuine sharing. This eventually brings suffering upon ourselves. False freedom can also bring many problems, such as dissent and disharmony among family and friends, but if we are generous and sharing, we create harmony and closeness, becoming much happier as a result.

True freedom comes from total independence. This does not mean rejecting everyone around us and putting a distance between ourselves and others, rather, it means being in control of our own minds and therefore being free from reacting impulsively or automatically to external events. It is important to stress that I am referring to both good and bad external events, because true freedom means being in control of our mind and our emotions *all of the time*, whatever happens. This is a difficult concept to grasp, especially for young people, but just remember that if we are easily swept away by external events and the emotions these generate, then we are a prisoner to these events and our freedom will always be limited.

REFLECTION—MAKING DECISIONS

Think of any big decisions you have made recently. How did you make them? Did you ask other people who have plenty of life experience for advice? Did you thoroughly consider all the consequences of your decision?

Were your expectations realistic or unrealistic? Did you consider the worst case scenario? Did you have any back-up plans? Were you completely honest with yourself, or did you make the decision because you wanted to impress someone? Did you consider all possible options?

Now think of any decisions you are about to make. Again, ask yourself all these questions, making sure you consider all your options carefully. Now sit upright with your spine straight, relax your body, take a few big deep breaths and make your mind clear. If you are honest with yourself, what is the best decision?

A Second Chance to Develop Wisdom

If we are seeking a happy and meaningful life, it is crucial to understand and remember the causes and conditions of happiness. Happiness and unhappiness are not random states—nor do they depend on good or bad luck. While external events may contribute to our happiness, fundamentally it depends upon our inner self. Happiness can only be ours if we possess the right mental attitude, and this comes from developing wholesome mental qualities.

A very small proportion of people naturally have the right mental attitude. These people are much happier and much more resilient than others in the face of difficulties; they also tend to experience far fewer negative emotions such as depression. Most of us, however, do not naturally have this attitude, and so we must consciously apply ourselves to developing it, especially by cultivating qualities such as gratitude and compassion. With constant and dedicated effort, we can gradually develop a mind which is peaceful and content, regardless of our external situation.

As a young adult who is developing independence and discovering how we can make a mark on the world, we are faced with many important decisions in life, love and relationships. I will therefore speak about some of these issues as well as the mental qualities that are most important at this age.

RESPONSIBILITIES AND DECISIONS

At this point in our life we are completely responsible for our future wellbeing, so we have great potential to achieve something if we have strong drive and determination. Sometimes we can feel overwhelmed when it comes to choosing where to direct our efforts and activities. For this reason I would like to suggest some guidelines, and especially mention some important external conditions that we should aim for when trying to live a peaceful and happy life. These are Buddhist ideas but they can be applied to anyone's circumstances. It may be helpful to think about them when deciding on the kind of lifestyle and career you wish to pursue, as well as the goals you wish to set for your life.

1. A Sufficient Income

So long as we are not living the life of a total renunciate, turning away from all worldly goals, we must have some degree of wealth in order to provide for ourselves. If we are able to save some money and accumulate wealth and property in a wholesome way, we will be able to enjoy future security. It is important, however, that we do this without becoming involved in any illegal trades or harmful professions. A harmful profession might include running an abattoir or commercial fishing enterprise, working in a lab where we are responsible for killing many animals or being a general in an army at war. If we have no choice but to be involved in this type of work, or our motivation is essentially pure, the consequences will not be so great, otherwise, engaging in this type of work is very likely to be detrimental to our long-term happiness, even though we may not initially notice this. Illegal trades such as dealing in drugs, weaponry or stolen goods also disturb our mental peace and are an obstacle to future happiness.

2. Wise Handling of Finances

It is important that we spend our money in profitable ways, looking after our family members and performing meritorious deeds. Those who are miserly are very attached to money and have difficulty spending it. Even if they buy something, they think continuously about the money it cost them and never get a real chance to enjoy what they have purchased. Many people spend money on unnecessary things just to feel good or to satisfy momentary desires, yet this habit is usually based on greed or impulsiveness and is likely to rob them of future happiness. Instead, it is important to prioritise how we spend our money, show genuine appreciation for whatever we have purchased and be mindful of how we can avoid supporting harmful institutions and environmental destruction. In addition, we should consider carefully how best to invest any savings that we accumulate, and it is certainly a good idea to discuss this matter with people who are skilled at handling finances. Money often has a negative connotation yet there is nothing wrong with money itself; indeed it can be very beneficial. The only problem is how we view or use it.

3. Freedom from Debt

If we are indebted to others, financially or otherwise, we may not have much peace of mind until the debt has been cleared. Often people go into debt to attain temporary happiness, but then the debt gets out of proportion compared to the amount of income they earn. This creates many difficulties in the longer term, and the interest we have to pay back on our credit card forces us to work even harder. Sometimes if we could see this debt visually it would look like a mountain! Even if we are a generous and kind person and go into debt spending money on others, this is an unwise way to give, as the interest we pay could serve a much more beneficial purpose.

4. A Harmless Life

If we have wronged or harmed anyone, we cannot enjoy any kind of satisfaction when we think of our deeds. The consequences of harming others always come back to us sooner or later just like a boomerang, whether this be physically or mentally. Sometimes these consequences occur in an obvious way, while at other times they are more obscure. Even at our deathbed we will not be able to escape the consequences of our actions, and we will find peace of mind hard to come by if we have not led a harmless life.

CHOOSING BETWEEN A SPIRITUAL AND A SECULAR LIFE

As I mentioned earlier, there are countless opportunities and paths we may choose to follow in our lives. There are, however, essentially two main pathways we must decide between—the spiritual life and the secular life. If we choose the secular life we must decide on life with a partner or a life alone.

I will not say a great deal about the spiritual life at this point as it would probably seem a little bizarre or unrealistic for most young people in today's modern world. Essentially, a spiritual life is a life devoted to finding inner peace and complete freedom from all our uncontrolled thoughts and emotions, however, it is also a life in which we must be willing to forgo all worldly attachments, many of which we take for granted, in order to concentrate intensely on spiritual practice under the guidance of a qualified teacher. If this is a path we wish to pursue then it is something that must be undertaken with the utmost care. We should not spend our whole life shopping around, taking bits and pieces from different religions and practices. Instead it is crucial that we find an authentic, proven spiritual tradition and a well-credentialed, authentic spiritual guide and community.

Fortunately, the great wisdom traditions of the world offer a variety of paths suited to people with different inclinations and abilities—those who are more intellectually inclined, those with a natural devotion, or those who find it easy to meditate. In our culture it may be possible for some people to engage fully in a spiritual life while at the same time holding down a job and having a partner, choosing to simplify one's life and trying to integrate this with spiritual practice. For others, it may be more suitable to join a spiritual community more removed from the busy pace of everyday life, or even to consider entering a monastery. I will speak more about the spiritual life in the next chapter, based on my own experiences in Tibet.

If this type of life seems too unconventional for us, there are plenty of opportunities to pursue happiness through a secular life. This does not mean we cannot have a spiritual dimension to our life; however, we won't be able to pursue this nearly as deeply as someone who makes it the main focus of their entire life.

If we choose the secular life, as the vast majority of people do, the biggest decision we will make is whether to seek life with a partner or as a single person. If we wish to have a partner, we should carefully consider the type of person we would like to spend our life with. We should be prepared to accept people as they are, as we all have faults. Don't expect to find someone who is perfect, or faultless, or who is just like yourself, and don't expect to change them later when you find they are not faultless. We should reflect honestly on our own experiences and personality type and observe those around us.

We may be a highly independent or ambitious person who wishes to achieve many things. Perhaps we wish to lead a simple and peaceful life, or a life which is always open to new opportunities. If this is the case, we may be more suited to a single life. With much less need to compromise, we will have much more space in our life. Without the responsibility or need to devote large amounts of time to family matters, we will have more opportunities and freedom to pursue our own interests

If we are a naturally thoughtful and caring person and wish to dedicate our life to another person and to raising a family, we may be better suited to a life with a partner—we will then have more opportunities to develop these qualities and lead a fulfilling family life. Most people wish to be close and intimate with someone else, and will therefore be drawn to finding another person they can completely trust and accept, providing a source of love and security. This can bring a much more powerful kind of happiness than can be found through wealth, fame or material possessions, as there will always be love and security, even when circumstances are not so great.

WHAT TO LOOK FOR IN A PARTNER

If we choose to spend our life with a partner, it is essential to know the most important qualities to look for in them. We must take care not to simply follow fleeting emotions or blind attraction,[19] as these kinds of feelings are only temporary and there is no guarantee that they will last for very long. When the honeymoon period of our relationship is over, there may be nothing to hold it together. If, on the other hand, we choose our partner because he or she has the right inner qualities, we are then laying the foundation for a stronger, more enduring kind of love and a happy life together.

This does not mean that 'chemistry' or 'zing' are not important. In fact, a certain type of energy can be felt between a male and a female with opposite sexual polarities, and we can learn to use this knowledge to our advantage. Most commonly, a man with a strong masculine quality, with a strong sense of direction and purpose, will be attracted to a female with a strong feminine quality, who is moved by her desire to share love and energy with others. Understanding this natural polarity can bring energy and passion to an intimate relationship. It can also help a couple work well together as a team and resolve many of the conflicts which arise.

Some people experience an immediate and long-lasting attraction to each other that goes beyond rational thought to a deeper level of feeling and intuition, as we hear about in the western concept of 'soul mates', however, this immediate kind of intuition and feeling of connection is not generally a sound basis for choosing a partner on its own, and it is important to combine this with reason. It is therefore essential to carefully reflect upon the inner qualities that we value in a relationship, in order to find a partner who is most suitable for us.

Here is a list of sixteen qualities to consider carefully when looking for a partner, beginning with the most essential ones:

A. Inner Qualities

A Good Heart

The most important quality to look for is a good heart. We should ask ourselves if he or she is a naturally loving and compassionate person. If your partner doesn't have a good heart, regardless of what other qualities they possess, you are unlikely to be happy with this person. Remember that anything could happen between you and your partner because circumstances can change at any time. A relationship in which both partners have a good heart will be able to weather these changes in the best possible way.

Faithfulness

The next most important quality is faithfulness. If you and your partner are not faithful to each other, many types of problems are likely to surface. If you cannot trust each other completely, you cannot love each other completely either.

Empathy

This refers to a genuine sense of understanding and sensitivity, being able to place oneself in the other person's shoes. If this is lacking, all kinds of conflicts will arise and it will be difficult to resolve them.

Good Communication

This is important because, even if your partner isn't naturally sensitive or understanding, a good ability to communicate can prevent misunderstandings and make conflicts easier to resolve. This includes both verbal and non-verbal communication. In this way you will be able to move more effectively from 'gridlock' to dialogue. Good communication can also help you to work well together as a team.

Honesty

Without honesty, we will find it very hard to place trust in the other person. It is impossible to hide something from our partner in the long run. If they find out, we risk losing their trust, regardless of how honest we usually are.

Similar Beliefs and Interests

It is quite important to have similar beliefs and interests. If your religious or political views are alike and your ideas about life are similar, living together will be easier and you will be able to know each other more intimately. Having similar likes and dislikes makes it easier to spend time together doing things you enjoy, rather than getting bored or irritated with one another!

Common Ambitions

This is crucial if you are aiming to achieve something together, such as owning a house or starting a family. Without goals that are at least similar it is easy to give up half way and fail to actualise the things we set out to achieve.

Intelligence

This quality is important if we are to effectively navigate through difficult periods in life and when we are faced with major decisions. With the help of an intelligent partner we are more likely to make wise decisions.

Being Practical

A practical person is very helpful to have around when it comes to everyday needs such as finances and other family matters. Sometimes we are reluctant to face the realities of life, overwhelmed with our situation or preferring to fantasise about something else. A practical person can help bring us back down to earth.

B. Other Important Things to Consider when Looking for a Partner

Good Health

If we choose a partner based on physical attraction or fleeting emotions and do not consider the quality of their health, we may end up disappointed if our partner is always unwell and find it burdensome to look after them. Viewed in another way, however, this may present an excellent opportunity to develop tolerance and compassion.

Good Education and Career

A trained mind that is oriented towards achievement can be helpful in taking care of problems that arise in life. However, we generally place too much value on education and career achievement, viewing them as symbols of high status or good rank in society. We should be sure not to choose a partner of high status just to 'show off'—this will cause us unhappiness in the long run.

Similar Cultural Background

If two people have a similar cultural background their habits will be similar, so they may find it easier to get along with each other. However, a similar cultural background is not imperative since habits are able to be changed. What is more important is that both of you are willing to learn and adapt to each other rather than stubbornly remaining entrenched in your own ways.

Family

Often we think marriage or family will make us happy. If we have a family which is close and caring, in which love is shared unconditionally, we will have a great advantage in life, however, if we fail to develop closeness and caring within the family unit, or fail to teach our children self-discipline, family life can instead be riddled with conflict.

Beauty

This is a lot further down the list than most people might imagine when considering what is important in a partner. In the same way that we may be proud to have a partner with a good career, we may think that having a beautiful partner will make us feel good about ourselves or impress others. Unfortunately, choosing to be with someone just because they look like attractive can lead to jealousy, insecurity and eventually unhappiness when the initial attraction has faded away. Remember also that beauty is in the eye of the beholder. If we develop genuine love for our partner we will see them as beautiful no matter what they look like.

Wealth

Choosing a partner who is financially well off can help us achieve a comfortable life, make many friends and relieve the stress of financial burdens. Ultimately, however, on its own this does not bring happiness and peace. Wealth can even create more trouble and take away our freedom, especially if we don't use it in the right way or take it for granted. The quantity of wealth is therefore not nearly as important as our ability to use the wealth we do have in a wise or compassionate manner.

Age

Some people think age is an important factor to consider, though it isn't nearly as important as many would make out. If you develop genuine trust and love, and have a similar level of wisdom, there is no problem with a large age gap. A significant gap however (for example, where a new wife is younger than the daughter from a previous relationship), often means there are different expectations and outlooks on life. This can lead to conflict, so it is sometimes better to avoid such a large age discrepancy.

When we are looking for a partner, all of these qualities need to be weighed up carefully. We should choose a partner who possesses more of those good qualities which appear earlier on the list (which are most important), and with whom we feel comfortable working together as a 'team'. The most crucial factor, however, is our intention to give pure love and take care of the other person. If we are only looking at the other person's qualities to fulfil our own needs or create a good image for ourselves, our expectations may not be met and problems are likely to arise.

It is also crucial to be comfortable 'being yourself' around your partner, rather than trying to live up to a particular image. In other words, you are willing to be honest and open about everything. Although it may take a little practise, it is possible to create a space where you both have nothing to hide and true intimacy can blossom, naturally and spontaneously.

HAPPINESS IN OUR RELATIONSHIP

A young man who had been married for a few years came to his grandfather for advice. He was unhappy in his marriage, he said, and wanted to end it. The grandfather told the young man that he should wait for two months and during this time treat his wife like an absolute princess. Though the young man was not happy about this, he agreed to it. Two months later, the grandfather asked the young man whether it was still his intention to get a divorce from his wife. 'Divorce?' the young man exclaimed, looking surprised. 'Why would I want to do that? I'm married to an absolute princess!'

This story shows us that how we perceive our situation depends on how we train our mental attitude. If we train ourselves to think our partner is a prince or princess, then this may well become our reality. No matter what situation we find ourselves in, the best condition for a happy and healthy relationship is to regard our partner as precious and take care of them in the best possible way.

This does not mean, however, that we can make any relationship work out perfectly if only we try hard enough. Rather, our aim should be to create a situation where the positive thoughts and feelings we have for each other greatly surpass the negative ones (which every couple has). This is what makes a couple better understand, honour and respect each other and their relationship, and we can say that such a couple is 'emotionally intelligent'.[20]

When we are in a relationship, it is important to be flexible and willing to change some of the personal habits our partner doesn't like. We also have to learn how to accept our partner's habits, even if they are annoying and require much patience and forgiveness on our part. Often we need to draw more on patience and forgiveness as we go deeper into a relationship as the initial euphoria and 'shine' usually wears away at some point and we inevitably begin to notice faults. In some cases, not only do we need patience and forgiveness but also great skill in helping the other person overcome their weaknesses.

In Tibetan Buddhist culture, a spiritual teacher always points out a student's weaknesses and sometimes even exaggerates these to the point of humiliation; but this is only done to the students who have the greatest potential. This technique usually spells disaster in a personal relationship, and even if we have the best of intentions, we should remember that direct confrontation seldom works, unless we are very skilful in our technique or our relationship has a very strong foundation. Additionally, before we try to help our partner with his or her weaknesses, we need to fully understand our own weaknesses and how difficult it is to overcome them.

We must keep in mind that it is easy to attribute the behaviour of another to their personal faults when it is actually due to something else. We should try to avoid this wherever possible, as we are really just guessing or imagining why the other person is behaving in a particular way. Instead, it is necessary to communicate well and clarify their reason for behaving the way they are, putting yourself in their shoes, however, do not expect to hear what you want to hear—be prepared to hear anything and be patient, with the determination to resolve the problem regardless of the difficultly or time required. If your partner seems irrational or unreasonable, remember this is not the reality of the heart. Let wisdom and compassionate awareness guide you towards the best course of action – more often than not a solution or a compromise can be found, yet if this is not the case you may need to accept what cannot be changed.

Not surprisingly, these principles apply not only to the relationship with our partner or spouse but to any relationship—with family, friends, business partners or neighbours. The ultimate source of conflict is too much focus on oneself and lack of consideration for the other. This is, however, rarely intentional. We are all aware that it is undesirable to be selfish, while being thoughtful and caring is good, yet we still have a deeply engrained habit of focusing on ourselves, partly derived from our culture and upbringing. The only way to overcome this habit is to shine the light of awareness on our actions throughout the day, reflecting carefully upon how we think, speak and act. Are we being caring or thoughtful? Can we improve our actions in any way? Can we say that we are acting in a way that is 'emotionally mature'? Gradually we can discover a person who is less self-centred, more compassionate and more likeable.

FALLING IN LOVE AND BROKEN HEARTS

I have discussed at great length the important qualities we should weigh up when selecting a partner, rather than simply choosing someone because we 'fall in love' with them. Although this may seem a strange concept to many people in the modern world, I believe much pain and emotional suffering can be avoided if we learn to view the topic of love from a more mature and grounded perspective.

It is certainly true that romantic love can be the most exhilarating and enjoyable feeling that anyone can experience. Anyone can share in this amazing state of bliss, regardless of their social status, creed or culture, or whether they are rich or poor. However, there is also a dark side to romantic love. We may think it will last forever, but this is not always the case. The bliss of romantic love may wear out after a few months or years, and the two people who could once not bear to be separated may suddenly find themselves jealous, angry or depressed. Furthermore, feelings of attraction may be unrequited, and this can also lead to inconsolable heartbreak. How, we may ask, can we learn to prevent or cope with these situations?

If the initial feeling which comes with falling in love lasted forever and always ended in happiness, it would be completely reasonable to choose a life partner on the basis of romantic love. For many people, however, this feeling only lasts for a short while and ends in unhappiness, even despair. Often the person they love does not feel the same way about them, yet they feel powerless in the face of the intense, uncontrollable longing they have for their loved one. I do not fully understand why people think falling in love is outside of their control. Certainly I believe falling in love is a very powerful emotion, yet any emotion, no matter what it is, is created by our minds. Because of this, we should be able to train our minds to deal with such emotions in a more constructive way.

I feel that many of our beliefs about love are culturally based, and I find it intriguing that there is no specific advice in western literature or psychology to teach people how to control falling in love. Western literature, songs and poetry have a very good understanding of the blissful, captivating feelings of romantic love, as well as the despair that comes with a broken heart, but there is very little advice on how to recover from a broken heart or how to prevent this from happening in the first place. Rather, literature and poetry seem to reinforce the attitude that falling in love is something completely beyond our control and that it is only human nature to be slaves to these emotions. Perhaps it would be more beneficial to ask ourselves how we can control these feelings, as falling in love does not always end in happiness and can even reinforce negative, possessive attitudes. Left unchecked, these attitudes can imprison us.

Having recognised the dark side of romantic love, what can we do about it?

Firstly, when looking for a partner it can be really helpful to keep in mind the inner qualities which they may or may not possess. Even if they are not physically attractive in the beginning, if they are rich in inner qualities they will become more attractive to you with time as the love you share increases. On the other hand, if physical attraction is the sole basis of your love, this can obscure your partner's inner characteristics, and their 'beauty' may fade away as problems come to the surface.

Secondly, we should realise that romantic love almost always contains an element of attachment which can cloud our judgment and lead to heartbreak later on. Recognising this is essential when we are looking for a partner. It is as though we were being carried downstream in a river and grabbed onto some reeds by the side of the river, thinking that we could climb onto the shore. Yet the reeds break off as they are not securely rooted on the river bank and we are carried away once again by the river. Similarly, we may think a relationship will bring us lasting happiness, yet if there is no foundation of unconditional love it will rarely work out this way. This does not mean, however, that every relationship based on romantic love is doomed to fail. If a relationship is built on genuine respect and unconditional love, then falling in love may well lead to lasting happiness.

It may be that we are in a relationship and suddenly realise we have very little in common with our partner. In this case it may be best to acknowledge these differences and agree to be practical and move on, especially if we have tried hard to find a compromise and none can be reached. Although this may sound a bit crazy, if we have true love and compassion for them we will be glad if they are happy, even if they do not want to be with us. We will realise this is true if we really learn to put ourselves in their shoes and consider their welfare above our own.

There is just one last thing to say on the matter of falling in love. There is a saying I have heard in the West, where people fall in love and then live 'happily ever after'. Let us pretend for a moment that this is at least partially true and a couple fall in love and then live happily together. Eventually, however, one of them will die. Of course we know that this is the reality of life, and it is this reality of impermanence that we must accept and deal with if we are truly to find happiness. I will talk more about this later in the book, but for now it is enough to realise that falling in love, like everything else in our lives, is impermanent—and may well be much more impermanent than many other things!

THE MANY DIFFERENT FACES OF LOVE

There are in fact many different forms of love, and romantic love is but one example of these. Love is something that all human beings have the capacity to experience, regardless of their language, culture or beliefs. Even if our experiences with love are limited, we still have an idea of what the word 'love' means, yet this word conjures up in each of us a different view of what love is or how it should be.

We can speak of five main types of love, most of which we will have experienced by this age: parental love, romantic love, endearing love, possessive love and compassionate love.

Each of these has a slightly different emphasis or value, yet they all share the same potential for compassionate love. This is the ultimate form of love, as lasting happiness is only achieved by cultivating this quality. It can be extremely useful to analyse the value and shortcomings of these various forms of love, as such awareness can help us identify how the love we have for others can be transformed into something even more rich and meaningful.

1. Parental Love

This is often known as 'mother's love' and describes a mother's love for her child. In the modern world we may also speak of 'father's love'. This type of love is imbued with patience, tolerance and nurturing. It is often regarded as 'unconditional', yet in reality this may not always be the case. It is usually strong and steady, often lasting a lifetime, and certainly does not rely on as many conditions as other forms of love. This brings joy and thoughtfulness, but also a sense of possessiveness at times, which can lead to much pain as our children struggle for independence and we realise we have very little control over how they choose to act. If we were to think of parental love in terms of percentages, we may have 50% compassion and caring, 20% ownership and about 30% attachment.

2. Romantic Love

This powerful and emotional form of love manifests as attraction, passion and adoration. As discussed above, it initially brings great joy, pride and inner strength. Sometimes it manifests as compassionate love but usually it is imbued with a self-centred and possessive attitude. For instance, we may be swept up in attachment to a person's appearance, reputation or image they present, leading to possessiveness, jealousy or anxiety. It is therefore nearly always a conditional form of love and is rarely long-lasting, especially if our relationship is based only on surface feelings.

Romantic love generally contains about 30% pride, 20% ownership, 30% clinging and 20% caring and compassion. As long as jealousy, possessiveness and self-centred attitudes predominate, this form of love is conditional and insecure. However, with a greater proportion of caring and compassion, self-centred concerns will evaporate and a deeper sense of happiness can be experienced. In this way romantic love can become unconditional.

3. Endearing Love

This form of love evokes warm feelings towards other living beings such as babies, animals and pets. We may also feel this while engaged with nature, art, music or anything which inspires such feelings. The experience of warmth that comes with endearing love is usually accompanied by a heartfelt sense of joy, and this does not depend on any specific conditions. Rather, it is associated with feelings such as protectiveness, softness and gentleness. Endearing love generally contains about 10% pride and ownership, 20%, clinging, 30% compassion and 40% caring.

4. Possessive Love

This form of love is associated with negative or destructive states of mind such as desire, envy, pride or feelings which are only superficial. An example would be the love of certain objects out of vanity or desire for self-gratification. This form of love contains around 50% ownership and pride, 30% clinging, 20% caring and almost no compassion.

5. Compassionate Love

This refers to genuine understanding, empathy and caring, or when a high proportion of these qualities exist. It is a feeling of love and caring for all living beings as equal to oneself, and does not mean feeling pity or sympathy towards others who are suffering. Rather it is genuine, non-judgemental, unconditional caring for all beings regardless of their appearance, status or circumstances.

Our capacity to embody compassionate love varies enormously. I believe everyone has a natural duty to develop this quality, as it is in the best interests of ourselves and others to do so. In particular, it can lead to higher degrees of happiness and strength; it may even help us achieve enlightenment. The cultivation of compassionate love normally requires a great degree of reflection and mind training; however, exceptional people have it in their hearts naturally.

The best compassion should be combined with wisdom; our caring for others can then become genuine, clear and indestructible. If we rely on sympathy or pity on its own, it is difficult to find a solution which truly benefits others. Rather we may end up feeling discouraged that our actions are not really effective, and our compassion may diminish even further.

How, then, can we develop compassionate love? It can be extremely helpful to identify which forms of love are present in our relationships and then strive to increase the proportion of compassion, respect and gratitude, while reducing the proportion of attachment, self-obsession and pride. Many aspects of our daily lives are influenced by a culture which fails to emphasise the importance of compassionate love. It is therefore crucial to practise this with our partners, families and those closest to us. With this foundation, we can extend unconditional love to all living beings with confidence that this will lead to a stronger mind and a happier life.

Thankfully there are many wonderful role models for the practice of this form of love. In the Buddhist tradition they are known as *Bodhisattvas*, beings who embody limitless, unconditional love for all living beings. Therefore, regardless of what they do, their lives are full of joy. Bodhisattva compassion is when genuine compassion is married with wisdom and is also known as 'warrior compassion', meaning there are no circumstances that can destroy or cause them to forsake this quality. Everyone should aspire to emulate this quality as we will never completely overcome suffering without it. We all have the potential to achieve this quality and therefore should try our best to cultivate it, regardless of the obstacles in our path.

ACHIEVING GOALS AND STRENGTH OF CHARACTER

Whichever stage we are at in our life, it is important to have goals, though this is of utmost importance when we are young and possess so much potential to apply ourselves towards attaining them. Goals can be both temporary, such as finishing a course of study, and long term, such as making an important discovery or spiritual development. Goals also need to be worthwhile. For example, buying an expensive house or boat will not ultimately help with future happiness, but a goal which involves helping other people will ultimately benefit both ourselves and others. Without goals which are realistic and worthwhile, we live life in a child-like or dream-like state and are in danger of just drifting along, never knowing in which direction we are heading and failing to realise our potential to make a difference in the world.

If we have worked out at least some goals in life, that is wonderful! This is the first crucial step, while the second crucial step is trying to fulfil these goals. The mental qualities we must cultivate to do this include ambition and enthusiastic diligence. Without these, any goal just becomes a fantasy.

It is also important to have strong belief in our ability to achieve the goals we set for ourselves. If we don't have total conviction in our ability to succeed, there will be a good chance that we will give up when discouraging circumstances arise. If, on the other hand, we have strong self-belief, then no matter what obstacles are in our way and no matter how many times we fail, we will always keep on trying and have a high chance of eventually succeeding.

The ability to keep persevering no matter what obstacles we are faced with ultimately boils down to strength of character. The cornerstone of a good, strong character is a combination of self-confidence, discipline and mental strength, along with a high degree of mental contentment. Some people are born with these characteristics, though most of us have to work hard at them, taking care that we do not develop one at the expense of another! By this I mean it is important to apply wisdom in how we develop our character. For example, when trying to develop self-confidence we may instead fall prey to pride or even arrogance, or when we try to develop mental contentment we may end up being complacent.

It is important to constantly monitor both our thoughts and our actions, and apply wisdom to the direction we are taking, externally and internally. This is where it is very useful to have a mentor or spiritual teacher to guide us in developing our mental qualities. It does not matter whether or not this 'mentor' has a religious background or a high level of education; the crucial point is that he or she is familiar with the good qualities we are talking about.

COMPLACENCY VERSUS CONTENTMENT

I wish to talk a little more about complacency at this point. I have already mentioned that when we speak of cultivating contentment, sometimes people confuse this with complacency. What do I mean by this? Take, for example, someone who hears that to achieve happiness we must cultivate our good inner qualities and learn to be content with what we have, instead of always wanting more. Unless we have good insight and wisdom or a good teacher, we may think all we need to do is have a positive attitude and not worry about anything. Unfortunately, this normally makes us lose focus and become disorganised. This is what I mean by complacency.

A complacent attitude will not help us achieve happiness. While having a relaxed and calm outlook can sometimes be beneficial, we can fall into the extreme of carelessness or being weak willed. Though it is important to be content with our circumstances, it is also crucial to realise the potential we have to change our situation by applying a little effort. It is possible to be content with what we have and where we are while still trying hard to achieve our goals. To give an example, if we are limited to having cold showers because the hot water system has broken down, we may be 'content' with cold showers for now and not let this disturb our mental peace—yet this doesn't mean we don't want to fix it! If we are too complacent then many opportunities are lost and our potential to improve ourselves may remain unrecognised.

While falling into complacency is one extreme leading us away from true contentment, the other extreme is the inability to be satisfied with our situation. No matter how good our external circumstances may appear, if we are always dissatisfied we will constantly want more and fail to appreciate what we already have. This attitude is often rooted in a mind-set of competitiveness and envy, wanting to be better than others or proud of our own achievements. Unfortunately this is often encouraged by the society in which we live.

Recently I read a revealing report which described a survey that asked people to respond to the following question: Would you rather be in a job where you earn $100,000 dollars per year and everyone else earns $80,000, or would you prefer a job where you earn $150,000 per year while others in your workplace earn $200,000? The answer seemed obvious to me, that most people would like to earn more money. However, the majority of people chose to earn less money, so long as they earned more than their co-workers!

I think this provides an important insight into human nature—that we like to be better than others and are dissatisfied when we are not. However, if we think having a million dollars would make us happy and we eventually reach this goal, we will not necessarily find happiness when we get there. Instead we may think that we need two million, five million or even ten million dollars to be happy! It is rare to find true contentment when our mind is focused on accumulating material wealth.

If we use the time we devote to earning money to developing self-discipline and contentment in our minds and hearts, our time may be better spent. By discovering the wealth of contentment, we would be happy all along, having found a true source of wealth. Furthermore, we are more likely to be healthy because a contented mind brings peace, and as many scientific studies now show, a peaceful mind is necessary for a healthy body. A healthy, stress-free mind, for example, can lead to reduced blood pressure and heart rate, improved immune function and benefits in a wide range of conditions,[21] including heart disease, diabetes and cancer. So contentment is not only good for the mind, but also for the body.

THE WHAT AND WHY OF COMPASSION

Everyone is familiar with the word 'compassion' and agrees it is a good thing. So why do we struggle to achieve it? Although people may mention compassion just about every day, our society encourages us to focus primarily on ourselves, and while we may hear about empathy and compassion, we are not usually trained to develop these qualities or the skills to maintain them. Even if we occasionally hear of the advantages of practising compassion, we seldom understand its true meaning and we rarely appreciate the short- and long-term benefits this can bring.

Many people think compassion applies only to situations where people are suffering, and that it means feeling sad and miserable for the person who is suffering. To feel sorry for a person who is suffering is important and is a good first step, but it is a long way from genuine compassion, where we are completely ready to act on this feeling. This doesn't mean making ourselves suffer in the place of others, but rather preparing the mind to be ready to remove other people's suffering, regardless of how difficult this may be. We can then act on this motivation to help others who are physically suffering, or perhaps by encouraging others to think in more skilful ways if they are suffering mentally. If we have this pure intention or quality in our mind, we will be blessed with a sense of inner peace and resilience, being far less concerned with our own problems.

Most human beings, whether religious or not, agree that compassion is a very important virtue, but when we look closely we can see there are many different levels of compassion.

The first level is when we are moved by seeing other people close to us suffer. For example, if a friend of ours is involved in a car crash that leaves him or her no longer able to walk, or we know someone who is dying from cancer, we are then motivated to do our best to help comfort them in this situation.

The second level is to be moved by the suffering of all human beings, including people from all religions and all walks of life. If we hear about an earthquake on the news, even though we don't know the victims, we may be moved to do what we can to help them. If we hear about the consequences of global warming, we can develop compassion for all the people who will be affected.

The next level is to develop compassion for all beings without any bias. We realise that all beings, including our enemies and those who act badly, desire to be happy and avoid suffering just like ourselves, and so we feel compassion for them just as we do for those near to us, understanding that they do not have freedom from their weaknesses. Not only human beings, but all animals, which also have the ability to experience pleasure and pain, become an object of our compassion. So if we see a spider or mosquito, we don't simply kill it because we find it irritating. Instead we are intensely aware of its right to life.

The fourth level of compassion is based on the profound wisdom which makes us aware of the deeper causes of suffering, not just the actual suffering we see around us. Although all living beings wish to be happy, we realise that through ignorance and unskilful actions, they continually create the causes of suffering for themselves. Why does an alcoholic get drunk and act irresponsibly, or a thief or murderer act the way they do? Though we may say they are 'addicted', they are still seeking some type of satisfaction or fulfilment, but are creating suffering for themselves and others with their unskilful actions. As they cannot see this, the root cause of their suffering is ignorance.

People who are rich and famous are also not immune to suffering. They suffer when the conditions that bring about their good fortune run out. Not only this, but at each moment they always have something to worry about; perhaps they are dissatisfied with their appearance or jealous of some popular new celebrity. They also have family that they worry about, such as elderly parents or their children. Therefore, no matter how good or bad a person's situation seems, they are still not free from suffering. If we think deeply, we see that practically everyone is continually immersed in some kind of suffering or is creating the causes for future suffering. With this understanding, our compassion becomes still more profound.

Finally, the highest level of compassion is based on an understanding of selflessness,[22] which means we see that everything is interdependent and insubstantial, with nothing truly existing by itself. This is a vast and profound idea which is the essence of Buddhist philosophy. To give a flavour of this understanding, imagine that we can read the mind of someone dreaming, who we can see is suffering terribly in a hellish environment. We know this is just a dream they have created in their mind, but they don't know this, and we wish more than anything else to wake them up from their dream because we can see directly their incredible potential for happiness if they could only realise the dream is not true. With this realisation, a profound level of compassion will spontaneously arise.

From another angle, to understand selflessness means to realise there is no innately existing 'I' and 'other'. As the barrier between ourselves and others melts away, our own happiness is not more important than the happiness of others. Compassion for all beings then just occurs naturally. This is not easy for everyone to comprehend, but from time to time we may have a glimpse of it through direct experience.

How is a deeper understanding of compassion practical in our everyday lives? Imagine we suddenly have an argument with someone. We may think that they are a bad person; they are wrong and we are right; and at that moment we might feel a strong sense of a separate 'I' and 'other'. However, if we analyse the situation closely and put ourselves in their shoes, we will find there are many causes and conditions we have not taken into account when jumping to the conclusion that our opponent is 'wrong'. We will discover many factors contributing to the events leading up to the argument. We might find that they have had a bad day, that we are also at fault, or that there is a huge misunderstanding at the root of the conflict.

When we appreciate that there is always a vast network of interdependent factors at play, we see reality much more clearly and come closer to understanding the truth of selflessness. There is no longer a basis for anger; instead we have a natural empathy and patience, realising that both of us just want to be happy and therefore any conflict is pointless.

If we truly understand that every living being is looking for happiness and trying to avoid suffering *just like ourselves*, then our compassion will be stable, without any boundaries. This is difficult to achieve, however, and in practice our compassion will be limited at times. Even if this is the case, practising any level of compassion is still beneficial. Remember it may take many years to develop a genuinely stable and unbiased sense of compassion. We must also keep in mind that compassion is not just feeling sad when others suffer, but also a sensitivity which allows us to *understand* others. Compassion and sensitivity therefore bring openness and closeness with others.

GENEROSITY, PATIENCE AND GRATITUDE

A natural way to express compassion is by being generous, patient and showing a sense of gratitude for whatever we have. During early adulthood especially, these actions steer us powerfully towards a happy, fulfilling and meaningful life.

Being generous does not mean giving away all our belongings to others. It means training oneself to avoid greed or laziness and being mentally prepared and willing to assist others by giving material objects, time and other forms of assistance when necessary. Being generous also means being patient, being able to forgive, and readily letting go of anger or resentment.

Patience means that when someone is angry with us or treats us unreasonably, we do not react negatively but react with calmness, reason and compassion. It also includes persistence in achieving our goals, even when confronted with hardships. Patience does not mean just idly waiting for events to take place without looking for alternative solutions, or just accepting adverse circumstances without attempting to change our situation. That would be complacency.

Athletes train their bodies with great patience, and they are generally much happier than those who are idle. The benefits and value of training our mind in patience and generosity will be far greater than that obtained by athletes. It is especially beneficial to practise patience and generosity with our speech and actions in our everyday lives. We can then develop a natural sense that these qualities are always there with us. After a while, living in this way becomes an immense source of joy. Remember that although it appears we are being patient or generous for the benefit of someone else, it is difficult to predict how much they will benefit by our actions. We, on the other hand, will always benefit

Most of the dissatisfaction and unhappiness we experience in our lives stems from a lack of appreciation of the precious things we already have. For instance, when we are healthy we forget to appreciate our mental faculties, our ability to see and hear, or our physical capabilities. We forget to be grateful for our precious human existence when everything is going well, yet when we find out we have cancer or some other serious illness, we suddenly realise how fortunate we were. Everyone who suffers a trauma or illness recognises the preciousness of their previous good health. It is better to learn to appreciate good health every day and experience that happiness now rather than waiting for some future misfortune to teach us this lesson.

If we reflect carefully, we will discover there are many things we can be grateful for. Yet more than anything else, it is the people near and dear to us who really deserve our gratitude. There is a story from the Buddha's time which illustrates this:

The Buddha once met a merchant called Sigala,[23] whom he saw bowing to the six directions of East, West, South, North, Down, and Up. The Buddha asked Sigala why he performed this ritual, and he replied that his father had told him to bow in the six directions every morning, though he did not know the purpose for this. The Buddha replied, 'Bowing is a practice which can bring happiness both in the present and in the future.' He told Sigala that he could contemplate gratitude to his parents when bowing to the East and gratitude to his teachers when he bowed to the South. Bowing to the West he could contemplate gratitude for his family, and bowing to the North he could contemplate gratitude for his friends. Bowing down, he could contemplate gratitude for his co-workers, and finally, bowing up he could contemplate gratitude to all wise and virtuous persons.

THE NEED TO TRAIN THE MIND TO DEVELOP INNER QUALITIES

At this point I wish to reiterate the importance of making a diligent effort to cultivate the inner qualities which lead to happiness, rather than relying on factors which are external and beyond our control. Everyone wishes to experience happiness all the time, yet this depends on what extent we are willing to go to cultivate the primary conditions for happiness.

There is nothing wrong with working towards achieving secondary conditions of happiness such as education, career, relationships or holidays. But what is most important is to recognise the primary conditions of happiness, which are found in our mental qualities, and to practise them genuinely. Why is this? Firstly, it is extremely hard to make all our circumstances perfect, and even if we were able to achieve the perfect circumstances right now, we might very soon become dissatisfied with what we had if we had not developed our inner qualities.

If we have not developed gratitude, we may be blind to the good fortune we already possess and find very little happiness even in the most fortunate of circumstances. If we lack discipline, we may easily get bored and lose focus when circumstances are not to our liking. If we haven't developed patience, we will lose our calm and peace of mind when confronted with difficult situations, therefore, the more we depend upon external circumstances for our happiness rather than these inner qualities, the more sensitive we become to even the slightest hardship. We get into the habit of dwelling on unfortunate situations and find it difficult to appreciate and enjoy good fortune when it comes our way.

In general, training our minds to adopt new mental qualities involves three steps. First we must familiarise ourselves with the advantages of the new habit we wish to adopt and the disadvantages of the old ways we seek to abandon. We must then commit ourselves to a ritual of self-reflection, spending short regular periods throughout the day familiarising ourselves with the new habit. Finally, we must *internalise* our awareness of the new habit, making it a part of us which is present constantly. For example, if we wish to improve our compassion, we can reflect on how training our mind in this way can help us develop inner strength and contentment and improve our relationships with others. We should then make a daily commitment to reflect upon and practise compassion whenever the opportunity arises. Through this daily exercise, over a period of months or years, our hearts will expand so that compassion becomes an unshakeable part of our life.

It is easy to think that we understand something if it appears obvious or easily makes sense to us. Our minds, however, are like leaves being swept along by the wind in many different directions, and listening to or reading something just once will not be enough to change how we think or act. Therefore it is crucial to reflect again and again upon any teachings we wish to apply to our life, no matter how obvious they appear at first. We must also keep in mind that happiness is achieved incrementally, moment by moment, and experience by experience. It will not suddenly appear after a life changing event or revelation.

If, however, we consistently focus on developing inner qualities, then happiness can become a primary, stable and constant condition. We cannot lose this condition as long as we are alive, and no-one can take it away from us.

EXERCISE – REFLECTING ON YOUR DAY

Set aside about fifteen minutes each morning and each evening. In the morning session, check your attitude before starting the day. Did you appreciate that you were alive this morning, living in a country where the conditions make it so easy to live compared to some third world countries? Are you determined to use this day wisely and practise compassion however you can, being true to your deepest values? In your work and your relationships, are you willing to be patient if things don't work out the way you expect?

In the evening, reflect upon the day that has just passed. Think of the people you talked to, the places you visited, and both the good and bad things that happened. What can you be grateful for? You may like to write a list of five to ten things in a 'gratitude journal'.

Sit up with your back straight, relax all your muscles, and take a few big deep breaths. Try to rest in a natural feeling of contentment and joy, and think about how you can make the next day truly meaningful and worthwhile.

The Age of Experience

People in the West are often quite negative about ageing, and many see this stage of life as the beginning of a downhill slope towards poor health and eventually death. In many ways, however, people in this age group are in a better position than a young person to attain happiness. This is because we have had a substantial amount of life experience by this age, and most people have managed to attain some wisdom, or at least we have encountered a great deal in our lives which we can reflect upon. Many people have undergone setbacks in their lives, especially financially, emotionally or physically, and so realise that they cannot rely on external conditions for happiness but instead need to find this within. With this knowledge we will find it much easier to cultivate the necessary internal qualities that lead to happiness.

When we reach this age, whether we are single or in a relationship, we will still be looking for happiness and seeking to avoid suffering. I have tried to identify the common problems faced by people of this age group and will attempt to provide some guidance for each of them.

THE SINGLE LIFE

If we are not married or in a long-term relationship at this stage of our life, this could be due to many reasons. We may have tried to live with one or several partners and for some reason these relationships did not work out, or our partner may have died. Perhaps we just never met the right person, or maybe we never wanted to be in a relationship in the first place. Regardless of the reason, many single people at this age feel lonely and out of place in a world where not having a partner can be seen as a failure.

If we look at this situation from a completely different angle, however, being single at this age can be seen as a wonderful opportunity. We have experienced many things and may have learnt from personal experience that many of the pursuits we devote our lives to are ultimately pointless or lacking in meaning. Pursuing a certain goal may have had a great deal of meaning for us in the past, yet we can sometimes have a sense that this has been 'accomplished' or we have learnt what we needed to learn, and that if we give ourselves a little space something new and more meaningful will emerge. This is like peeling an onion, layer by layer, so that we can gradually reveal a deeper purpose.

With this kind of wisdom to guide us, and with no partner, there are many opportunities that can open up for us. We may enrol in university and begin a new course of study. We may travel around the world, learn a new language, write a book or start a new business to serve our local community. Although it may seem unconventional, we could even enter a monastery or devote our life to gaining spiritual realisation, leading a simple life which allows us to truly develop peace of mind. We can do all these and many more wonderful things if we do not have a partner or family to whom we are responsible.

MONASTIC LIFE

The monastic life may sound like an unconventional idea to many people in the modern world. After all, we may imagine a sterile and boring existence, with nuns and monks cloistered away from the world, following strict rules and not being allowed to have any fun. I would like to mention a little bit about the Buddhist monastic life, as this may be quite different from what many people expect. I am certainly not trying to sell Buddhism as the 'best' religion or the 'best' way of life, rather I am purely wishing to share my own experience with the hope that you might find this useful. I have lived as a Buddhist monk for many years and therefore can tell you about this life with some confidence.

The true goal of a Buddhist monk is not to have a happy or pleasant life, but rather to reach enlightenment. However, if we spend our life working to reach a state of enlightenment, then a happy and peaceful life will naturally be ours. I often see unhappy and lonely men and women in the West, and I think what a wonderful opportunity this person would have to live a peaceful ordained life.

Why do I say this? The foundation of an ordained life is renunciation. When I was ordained I was only eighteen years old. I had not suffered heartbreak, financial difficulties or disappointment. I had only experienced enjoyable times with friends and family, and had even fallen in love—and I wanted more of this! I therefore should have found monastic life hard at first; however, I was still able to develop renunciation through the power of Buddhist practice. If, on the other hand, we have already experienced a broken heart and other disappointments, we can turn this to our advantage by letting these experiences inspire genuine renunciation.

What does it mean to devote our life to reaching enlightenment? Fundamentally, this idea is based on a teaching by the Buddha called *The Four Noble Truths*. The Buddha did not teach these truths in order to convert people to Buddhism, but rather to show every living being the way out of suffering. These truths therefore apply to everyone:

1. The nature of life is suffering or unsatisfactoriness.

2. Suffering is not random but has a cause—our negative emotions, our previous negative actions and our tendency to grasp onto an exaggerated idea of 'self' and 'other'.

3. Complete freedom from suffering, or enlightenment, is possible.

4. The path to enlightenment involves eliminating the causes of suffering by practising discipline, concentration and wisdom (also known as The Noble Eightfold Path). [24]

These truths are not just intellectual theories or philosophical speculation, but were discovered through the Buddha's direct experience in meditation. Many other meditators and contemplative practitioners since the Buddha's time have also reached the same experience, confirming these discoveries in much the same way as a scientist repeats an experiment many times in order to verify a scientific discovery. Furthermore, newcomers are encouraged not to accept any of these ideas with blind faith, but rather to thoroughly analyse and test them in their own experience, just as we may test gold for its purity.

The purpose of Buddhist monastic life, then, is to follow this well-proven path in an environment in which there are few distractions. This allows one to lead a simple life and focus the mind intently on eradicating the root causes of suffering, just like the Buddha and his many followers. Far from being a self-centred pursuit, the goal of this type of life is to increase our strength of mind so we can develop far greater capacity to help others. Only when we have understood how we ourselves can overcome suffering can we truly help others to do the same.

We often, therefore, speak of 'enlightenment for the sake of others'; from this perspective we are seeking much more than just our own salvation. In this way, many of the great Tibetan spiritual teachers of the last generation, such as my own teacher, Lama Lobsang Trinley and the great sixteenth Karmapa,[25] all devoted many years towards cultivating the mind of enlightenment. This involved removing themselves from the everyday world for several years to engage intensively in retreat practice, yet once they attained true realisation their ability to work for the benefit of others was extraordinary. This may also apply to great beings from other traditions such as Jesus Christ.

Buddhist monastic life is probably quite similar in all countries. As

I have only experienced the monastic life in Tibet, however, this is the only experience I can share. The first thing we should know is that if our motivation is pure then any monastery will welcome us to stay with them, and we may stay as long as we wish. The second thing is that if we are unable to support ourselves there is generally no obligation to pay for accommodation, food or other expenses. However, I am not advocating that we enter a monastery to escape from worldly responsibilities—it is crucial that our motivation is genuine, and since westerners are usually quite wealthy by Tibetan standards, it is only natural that we should be generous if we are able. It would be wrong to take advantage of the generosity of a monastery, and this could only lead to negative consequences.

I know many people who believe they do not have the right level of study or knowledge to join a monastery, yet this is a false assumption. As with any place of learning, those attending a monastery have attained varying levels, ranging from those monks or nuns who are easily distracted in their practice to those who have reached a level of excellence. Staying in a Buddhist monastery does not necessarily mean we have to devote all of our time to studying or practising Buddhism. Though we usually are obliged to adhere to a strict daily routine and maintain exemplary conduct, there is also a lot of time which we are free to use in a way best suited to our own interests and talents. We may, for example, prefer to help maintain the monastery's computers rather than study all the time.

Regardless of what role we play, however, there is no chance that we will experience loneliness or isolation. In the Tibetan language there is a word that can be translated as 'lonely', though most people don't fully understand what this means because they are so unfamiliar with this experience. In all honesty, I myself did not understand the meaning of loneliness or depression until I came to the West.

If we are considering a monastic life, we should familiarise ourselves with the many different monastic traditions that exist in the world today and ask ourselves what type of lifestyle would best suit our spiritual development. If, for example, we have been brought up a Christian and have strong faith in this tradition, it may suit us best to join a Christian monastic order. If we wish to focus more intensively on meditation practice, the Thai forest tradition of Theravada Buddhism or the Zen tradition may be good options to explore. Other traditions, meanwhile, place more emphasis on scholarship or community-based projects. It may be that we are drawn to joining a monastic community in a foreign country, yet learning a new language is a significant barrier. However, learning happens naturally once we are immersed in a new language, and after several years communication is rarely a problem.

Unfortunately western culture is often unaware of the value of spiritual development and the benefits of supporting this, so finding an authentic path which is supported financially can be difficult. Another option is therefore to become part of a group or lay com-munity. Nowadays a number of organisations provide support for people who wish to walk this path. Instead of wearing robes and abiding by the precepts of an ordained monk or nun, they live an 'outer life' which is similar to others, committing themselves to the discipline of work and family life, yet their inner life is different; they choose to simplify their lives to make space for meditation practice, the study of spiritual teachings and the commitment to embody these teachings in every aspect of their lives. They may also decide to set aside time for regular periods of retreat.

We must remember, however, that searching for an 'authentic path' is not something to be undertaken lightly; there are many 'spiritual teachers' who promise great things, yet with careful analysis we find their teachings lack authenticity, they are embroiled in controversy or there is an element of cult-like behaviour. The task of finding a suitable and effective path requires great skill and discernment,[26] careful reflection upon our own motivation, and brutal honesty. We must also be aware of our tendency to become attached to spiritual concepts or certain expectations, which can distract us from engaging properly in a spiritual life or finding an authentic path.

There is no guarantee that we will not meet with difficulties and misunderstandings, even once we have made a commitment to a particular path. We may, for example, encounter people who give us unhelpful or confusing advice or we may be discouraged when those around us do not practise what they preach. In this situation it is crucial to keep checking that our motivation is genuine, and to keep relying on our own common sense and good judgment rather than blind faith. If one path clearly doesn't suit us or benefit us, we should have the courage to leave, tactfully and gracefully. We should avoid being overly critical or seeking any form of retribution, as ultimately we may be harming ourselves. If our motivation is pure and authentic, and we have made an effort to study authentic teachings, it is only a matter of time before we meet an authentic teacher.

LIFE AS A LAY PERSON

Many people think or even dream about renouncing the world and entering a monastery, however, they often feel they have responsibilities that they simply cannot give up, for example to elderly parents or children. Nevertheless, if a person's renunciation is strong and pure, they may still be able to give up possessions, career and family to enter more fully into a spiritual life. This was often the case with the most exceptional Buddhist monks and also with the Buddha himself, who sacrificed his life of luxury, his position as heir to the throne, his wife and new son to attain enlightenment. So if the pull to monastic life is strong enough, my advice is that we should definitely go for it!

However, this does not mean we must devote our life to spiritual attainment in order to be happy. If we cannot relate to this idea, we then have a choice to look for a new partner or remain single. As mentioned previously, the single life offers many advantages, with many opportunities to study, travel, meet people and explore dif-ferent interests. Many doors are open and we certainly do not have to be lonely. By becoming involved in local groups or organisations we can feel part of a community and find companionship and friendship here. Yet if we are content to lead a simple and peaceful life, we do not necessarily need any goals or activities to keep us busy. Although we may be alone, we will never be lonely if we find true contentment within.

What if we have always wanted to marry but have never managed to find the right person? From a traditional Eastern point of view, by this age we may have 'missed the boat', yet nowadays people are getting married at every stage of life and age doesn't really matter all that much. Having a wiser, more mature perspective with plenty of life experiences under our belt, we are likely to make wiser decisions when it comes to relationships. However, there are also drawbacks. An older man who marries a young woman, for example, may feel insecure and jealous of younger men. The most crucial thing to remember is that whether we marry young or old, or indeed whether we marry at all, we can never say which is the better destiny and which path would bring us the most happiness. The conditions which bring happiness are cultivated from within and should not depend upon whether or not we have a partner.

ENTERING INTO A NEW RELATIONSHIP

If we decide to look for a partner at this age we will have much life experience to bring to the relationship. We may have had one or more previous relationships that have ended, and there may have been many reasons for this. Regardless of the conditions or circumstances leading to the end of these relationships (apart from death), the root cause is almost always a lack of unconditional love and compassion. Genuine love and compassion will not diminish with time, but will most likely deepen over the years. Other forms of love, on the other hand, are based more on attraction and fleeting emotions – this inevitably declines with time as wisdom and compassion are lacking.

We should reflect upon our previous relationships and ask ourselves what foundations they were built upon. Were they based on care, understanding, compassion and respect, or were they were based on self-centred needs and blind attraction? We can use this wisdom to lay a strong foundation for a new relationship. Essentially, we must check if we have the capacity to be generous, patient, thoughtful and compassionate, or at least recognise their importance. These inner qualities prepare us well for a happy new relationship. Otherwise we might fall back into old habits and repeat the mistakes of our past.

MAINTAINING A RELATIONSHIP

Although this is not a religious book, I would like to mention a specific Buddhist text, known as the Sigalovada Sutta,[27] which offers some simple and practical wisdom about how a husband and wife should treat one another. Basically, it advises a husband to be courteous, faithful and respectful to his wife and supply her needs, while a wife should be faithful to her husband and protect his property.

This text of course dates back to ancient times and assumes that the husband is the main income provider. The situation nowadays is a little more complicated, as often both husband and wife have a job. Although who should undertake most of the household duties and who should be the primary source of income is open to negotiation, the essential points that they should respect one another, be faithful to one another and take care of one another's needs, remain relevant to this day.

I also believe it is important for women and men to explore the basic differences between their genders. It is common knowledge in western psychology that men and women see the world in subtly different ways.[28] For example, men are generally more driven by a sense of direction and purpose, while women are moved by their desire to share love

117

and energy with others. When confronted with a problem, men might be inclined to withdraw or seek 'time-out' until they find a solution, while women would much rather talk about issues even if this does not solve the problem. My own experiences have also taught me that most women are better at multi-tasking. Gaining an awareness of these types of differences can help each partner recognise the other's strengths and limitations and divide household tasks accordingly.

No matter how well we understand the general differences between men and women, however, we still need to understand the specific personality and nature of our partner, and this requires good, open communication. It is all too easy to misinterpret our spouse's behaviour, and to avoid falling into this trap, it is important to be able to discuss, openly and with pure intention, why they might be acting in a particular way. Any conflict will be easier to resolve if we have a strong foundation of goodwill towards our partner, and especially if you both view conflict as an opportunity to learn and grow together.

This brings us again to the importance of pure or unconditional love in any marriage or partnership. To have pure love for someone is to want their happiness above our own. Many people say they love a person with all their heart and then become devastated when their partner decides to end the relationship. They may begin to say that they hate their former partner, eaten away by jealousy or resentment. This is an example of possessive love rather than pure love. If our love is pure, on the other hand, we should even be happy for them when they leave us for someone else if this makes them happier. Whenever I make this point in public talks many people are shocked and reluctant to agree with me. Yet pure love for another human being means we genuinely want the best for them, regardless of the effect this has on us. Perhaps we may think this kind of attitude is self-defeating and will fail to benefit us, however, loving someone with a truly pure motivation will definitely make our relationship stronger, and by cultivating this quality our mind will open to true happiness.

MAKING YOUR CHILDREN BETTER THAN YOURSELF

Everybody loves their children (with rare exceptions), yet often parents lack the know-how to train them effectively. Sadly, there are some parents who neglect their children's basic physical and emotional needs. At the other extreme, some parents will pander to their child's every desire. I have often heard people tell me how much they love their children, so much so that they cannot say no and give them everything they want!

Although these parents are trying to be kind, in truth they are really harming their children. The child who is given everything will often grow up expecting life to be easy and that they can immediately have whatever they desire. When they are faced with the realities of life, especially when they encounter disappointment and failure, they have difficulty coping because they have not learnt how to persevere or be patient. Parents should not be overly surprised by this; after all, you cannot grow a plant in a hothouse, place it outside in a winter storm and then be surprised if it does not survive. It is crucial, therefore, to set firm boundaries and teach children how to survive hardship, while at the same time showing them genuine love and compassion.

Setting consistent boundaries, such as saying no to watching TV or going to sleepovers and making them assist with the housework, not only teaches our children that life isn't always easy, but also provides a structure or rhythm to their lives which helps them feel secure. When our children don't have to deal with change and uncertainty all the time, they are able to develop good ethical conduct—not because they are forced to, but because they learn to see the benefit of having a good, disciplined routine. This also becomes a foundation for creativity, confidence and kindness in the presence of others.

Firm discipline and boundary setting are also crucial if we are to keep our children on a 'middle path'—they should not be allowed to get away with whatever they want, yet neither should they be pressured to live up to high expectations. In addition, when preparing our children for the future we should not only speak about the money we have put aside for them or the house we will buy for them. Certainly, this material assistance is useful, but of much greater importance is to invest in our children's mental and emotional development.

We should therefore remember the root conditions for happiness and teach these to our children—especially self-worth, compassion, self-control and strength of character. By teaching them wisdom and compassion through story-telling, conversation and the example of our own actions, we will prepare them in the best possible way for future happiness and success.

It is important to teach these qualities through all the ages of childhood,[29] remembering that demonstrating these qualities ourselves is always the best way. In the first four years of life, children are extremely sensitive to the emotional environment they grow up in, so the most important thing is to show our children complete unconditional love. We should try to make them feel they are truly special, filling them with a deep sense of inner worth. During primary school years, we should point out and support our children's creativity, hard work and helpfulness to others, encouraging all these qualities to blossom, then during their teenage years we can help them feel like a worthwhile and contributing member of the human race, knowing their lives have meaning whatever happens. Rearing a teenager is never easy as we are torn between wanting to do the best for them and learning to trust that they will find their own path. Learning to love them unconditionally, regardless of the choices they make, can certainly be a great challenge.

Finally, one of the most vital lessons to teach our children is the harmful consequences of drug, tobacco and alcohol use. Some parents think that because they may have smoked or experimented with drugs in their youth, they have no right to instruct their children not to do the same. This is not true—with your experience you will be able to teach your children more effectively and try to make them better than yourself. Remember, however, that if you are having difficulties managing your child's behaviour, you are never alone and help is always available.

PARENTS AND THE OPPORTUNITY TO SHOW GRATITUDE

By this stage in our life it is quite likely that our parents' health is declining or they may no longer even be alive. If they are in poor health they are likely to make many demands upon our time and resources. We may be summoned to take them to doctors' appointments, to help out with jobs they can no longer do, or they may even wish to move in with us so we can better look after them.

In Tibet it is expected that children will care for their parents in their own home when their parents are older. Although the culture is different in the West, it is still important to treat our parents in the best possible way. With rare exceptions they have been immensely kind to us and it is only natural that we wish to repay this kindness. Remember too that our children will learn from our example how parents should be treated—if we set a good example by looking after our parents in a kind and compassionate way, our children are more likely to do the same for us.

When parents get older and require our help, this can cause considerable anguish for those who have not had a good relationship with them. Maybe we feel that our parents never really cared for us, or maybe they were alcoholics or drug addicts. Perhaps they did not give us enough attention or failed to provide us with a good education or financial support. Whether or not they made mistakes with our upbringing, it is still natural that parents wish their children to have a happy life. We can understand this when we reflect upon our feelings towards our own children.

Since I have been in the West I have encountered many people who are not happy with their own lives and hold their parents responsible for this. They attribute their failure to have a successful life to their parents' failure to care for them. This view may originate from some branches of psychology that tell us that people's negative personality traits are strongly influenced by their upbringing and are very hard to change. From a Buddhist point of view, this is not quite true. Not every outcome in life is the result of our childhood experiences. Rather, we carry the seeds of our destiny within ourselves. Although we may feel 'stuck' in certain habits which we can trace back to certain childhood events, we can still learn to accept our situation and forgive those we might blame.

Let us assume for a moment that our parents *are* responsible for the failures in our life. Even if this were the case, there is no advantage in feeling anger, hatred or disappointment towards them, as these negative emotions would only be harming us. Once we are aware that holding onto anger achieves absolutely nothing, we can learn to compassionately accept the journey we have been through and move forward in the direction of our goals and dreams. Instead of harbouring anger, remember that gratitude is one of the essential conditions for happiness. We will naturally feel gratitude once our anger has been overcome, because the truth is that parents love and care for their children dearly, despite their imperfections. By feeling grateful to our parents for bringing us up, we cultivate happiness and inner freedom within ourselves.

UNSATISFYING JOBS AND THE TRAPS OF MATERIALISM

Many people I have spoken to seem unhappy because of their job. They tell me they are constantly rushed and stressed, they do not like the people they work with or they wish they could stop working. Although there are no easy answers, I believe it can be helpful to look carefully at our motivation for engaging in our particular field of work. Are we motivated by the desire to help people or to do something that we genuinely enjoy or find meaningful? Or are we simply striving to get ahead and earn a lot of money or attain high status? Is work simply a chore rather than a passion, little more than something to pay the bills, feed our family or support other interests?

If we see our work as a 'calling' or a way of sharing our unique gifts with the world, we are likely to derive great satisfaction from our work. If, on the other hand, we are driven by the desire to build a bigger house or get that prized promotion, our work can become an obsession, as we are spurred on by the desire to move 'up and on'. Even though we may enjoy what we do, the rest of our life is likely to suffer. Stress or even burn-out is often the result, since what goes up must come down. Alternatively, if our work is little more than a chore or obligation, we are also unlikely to find true satisfaction. It may take a great deal of soul-searching, then, to find something else that is true to our deepest purpose.

We should also be aware that work satisfaction depends little on the type of job we do.[30] For example, working as a cleaner might hold tremendous meaning for us, especially when we think that everyone appreciates cleanliness and we are making a contribution to the lives of others. In contrast, we may work as a doctor and feel frustrated or bored because our patients never cease complaining and we are not earning enough money.

If we really dislike our job, we need to seriously reconsider why we are doing it. If it is just to make money so we can afford to maintain a wealthy lifestyle, then it makes sense to simplify our life and reduce our desire for material wealth, opting for a job with fewer hours. We all have a tendency to think that acquiring more possessions will make us happier, yet rarely can we see that this is like trying to quench thirst with salty water. Just as we become even thirstier after drinking salty water, we become more and more dissatisfied if we only look outside ourselves to make us happy. A friend of mine who works as an engineer once told me he was not happy because all his friends earned more than he did. I mentioned that no matter how much he gets paid, someone else will always earn more. It is not easy to be content with our lot in life, and I can only wish that more people could taste the inner freedom and peace of mind that such an attitude brings.

Lacking a genuine or good motivation is certainly one reason for being unhappy at work, though another reason is that we may not possess enough ambition or focus. Sometimes Asian people are able to work over fourteen hours a day with the goal of quickly paying off a mortgage for a new home, for example. Their motivation may not necessarily be good and their lives may not be 'balanced', yet they are generally happy because they have trained their minds to have a high level of focus and engagement. They are content to put their head down and just do the work rather than worry about holidays, work conditions or other expectations. They are simply too busy to be sad or depressed.

This kind of work ethic may seem unbalanced from a western point of view. To a certain extent this is true, but we must remember that ambition, determination and focus are indirect causes of a certain level of happiness and therefore they have some value. However, we need a more balanced view to attain higher levels of happiness.

FREEDOM, SUFFERING AND IMPERMANENCE

In Buddhism we speak a great deal about freedom from suffering. However, this idea is often misunderstood, especially in the modern world. There are several different types of freedom. The first is external freedom, such as freedom of speech and freedom to live without fear of persecution. This kind of freedom is lacking in many places in the world. Nearly all Western countries are very fortunate to have this type of freedom, though it is rare for us to really appreciate this.

The second kind of freedom is individual freedom, which is valued very highly by many people in the post-modern West. With this kind of freedom we think, 'I have the right to do this or the right to own that'. We therefore take pride in the idea of complete freedom of individual behaviour, or autonomy.

Although it is important to make our own choices about how we live and act, this is not actually real freedom. This kind of attitude often makes us focus mostly on our own welfare, and as a consequence we create a distance between ourselves and others, for example our friends or neighbours. We may even avoid others altogether or fail to respond to others because we are so concerned about 'respecting their freedom'. For example, if a young man chooses to start smoking or act in a way which is clearly causing him harm, we may just think, 'That's okay, he is free to act in this way if he chooses'. This is not true freedom, but rather an unhelpful attitude that will eventually lead to loneliness. This is a common problem in the modern world and something we all need to seriously reflect upon.

What we may not realise is that false freedom can be very hard to recognise in the West, as it derives from centuries of cultural habituation. In Asian countries, for instance, people may fight with one another, but usually they are able to resolve conflicts and even grow closer to each other as a result. However, by avoiding conflict under the pretence of respecting another's rights, it is easy for us to grow distant and become less aware of the wellbeing of others.

Real freedom, on the other hand, is vital for happiness. This does not mean being able to do whatever we wish whenever we please, but rather being able to control our emotions and desires so that we can decide how to react in any situation and choose how to live our lives without being driven by emotional conflict. From a Buddhist perspective, this means we become free from karma, or free from the force of our past habits and actions. If we are free from karma, no matter what situation we encounter, we are not controlled by our emotions and habits. Then we are truly free.

Even if we are not Buddhist, being able to control our thoughts and emotions gives us great freedom. As I have said earlier, it is not external events which dictate how happy we are, but rather how we react to them, therefore, as our thoughts and emotions play such a big role in determining our level of happiness, having even a little control over them is extremely valuable.

As we get older we have more experiences in life, both good and bad. By the time we have reached this stage, we are likely to have witnessed suffering in some form, perhaps through the death of a loved one or the end of a relationship. We will therefore know that, despite the best health care, the best insurance policy and all the effort in the world, we can never stop death, disease, ageing, or the many other things in life which inevitably bring suffering. The nature of life is its impermanence—it is constantly changing in both good and bad ways.

If we hold on tightly to our feelings and to the people around us, then we create a world based on our own suffering and that of the people close to us. This is what the Buddha realised all those years ago. Some people become very depressed when they realise this and think, 'Well, what's the point? Since life is suffering, I may as well give up now'.

However, the Buddha showed us there is a way to break free from the cycle of suffering, and this is to let go of our attachment. This applies to both negative circumstances and emotions such as anger or hatred, as well as enjoyable circumstances and emotions which bring us pleasure, like romantic love. We need to realise that these will come and go, and while we can still enjoy pleasurable emotions, if we hold onto them too tightly then we suffer when circumstances change. Instead, we should aim to achieve the freedom which comes with a peaceful, happy and compassionate mind, not pulled this way or that by the whims of emotions and desires.

EXERCISE—LEARNING FROM LIFE EXPERIENCE

We have accumulated much in the way of life experience by now and we can learn many valuable lessons if we reflect deeply on what our lives have taught us. This may even make us re-evaluate some of our priorities.

First bring to mind a person you had a relationship with in the past. This does not necessarily have to be a partner— it can be a friend, a parent or

*perhaps a co-worker. What was your motivation for being in the relation-
ship? Did it work out the way you expected? How successful were you at
overcoming difficulties? How open was your communication? Perhaps if there
was a period of great difficulty you can write down what you remember—this
can help you accept the past and move on.*

*Then bring to mind a job you have had in the past and ask yourself similar
questions. What was your motivation for doing this kind of work? What
else did you learn from your experiences?*

*Now look at your present situation. Ask yourself, 'How can I apply the
lessons I have learnt? How can I live my life in the wisest possible way?'*

*Sit upright with your spine straight and your hands in your lap, tensing
your body and then feeling it relax all over. Ask yourself honestly if there is
anything you want to change at this stage of your life, and then think about
how you can make this happen.*

The Age of Wisdom

In this period, the fifth stage of life, there will be great differences in the conditions that people face, yet whether this period of life is joyful or not depends on how we view life and how broad or limited our perceptions are. It is a time when we complete many of life's obligations and also come to terms with many of the challenges we have faced throughout our lives. For some, their external conditions allow for a new beginning. They are finally able to retire from their job, set off to travel the world or spend more time with loved ones. For others, this stage of life may be marked by loss—loss of a spouse, loss of a role in society after retiring from a job, or loss of good health. Regardless of our situation, however, at this age we are entering a stage of life when self-reflection and finding a sense of meaning are important. In so doing we can learn to see that any kind of loss may in fact be an opportunity for spiritual growth and insight.

Human nature puts great value on achievement, competition and acquiring things, and we have probably strived for many things over the course of our life. We have probably worked hard to earn money, to acquire a house and other possessions, to raise our children and to main-tain a successful career and to win praise from others. Even at this age many people still continue to strive for such things. Think carefully about the life we have built up for ourselves. Do the things we have worked so hard for seem truly meaningful? Does our *life* seem meaningful to us? Have we developed inner security? Think about this in the context of growing older. Though we may have worked hard and achieved many things, all this time our body has been slowly and inevitably declining. By this age we will realise we can no longer deny the inevitability of death—no matter what we do, there is no escaping this. Does it still make sense to continue living our life in the same way? Or is it perhaps time to make some changes and establish some new priorities?

I believe most people will realise that many of the things they have filled their lives with no longer have the same meaning now that they are growing older. This does not need to be a depressing thought, however, and we certainly should not spend endless hours regretting how we have spent our time and energy. Rather, we can use this realisation as an opportunity to cut our attachment to many of the things we no longer find important, and to develop the wealth of inner contentment. This can open up a whole new world, and it can also give us an opportunity to pay more attention to our mind.

It is certainly not too late to develop our mind, and we do not need to become a monk or nun or spend hours in meditation every day to achieve this. At this stage in our life, as at every other stage, what is most important is to reflect on our attitudes and actions in our daily life. We will find there are many simple things we can implement to develop our inner qualities and promote our own happiness, no matter how good or bad our quality of life may be.

LOSS AND IMPERMANENCE

As mentioned earlier, many people see this age as the start of a decline and eventual loss of things they consider important. It is easy to delude ourselves into thinking we can control the world around us, believing we can rely on good medical care and insurance policies if things go wrong, however, this simply is not true. Even though we have been approaching death from the time we were born, often this only becomes clear to us as we face our own mortality, and sometimes it can come as quite a shock. We also come to realise that the time of death is not fixed, that whether we are a teenager or a ninety-year-old, we can never be assured that we will live to see another year.

Mental suffering can result from any kind of loss, such as loss of a loved one, loss of a job, loss of status or loss of health. All of these losses can cause us great suffering if we do not view them in a realistic way, so we then have a choice. We can either suffer uncontrollably when our conditions change and our loved ones die, or we can learn to accept that everything is impermanent, that old age, sickness and death are just a natural part of life,[31] not a conspiracy against us. We can then realise that holding on tightly to anything will only lead to suffering in the end. Through acknowledging impermanence, we can develop an entirely new outlook on life and prepare ourselves for loss, allowing us to maintain a happy and peaceful state of mind, whatever our external conditions.

DEATH OF A SPOUSE

For many people, the death of a husband or wife is the most devastating event that will happen in their lives. Although I have never been married, I think I have some understanding of a loss of this magnitude. In my youth I lost both my father and my brother, and in Tibetan culture the ties between father and son or between two brothers are almost as strong as the bond between husband and wife. I would therefore like to speak briefly about how we can cope with a loss of such magnitude.

When a loved one dies we must try to look outside our own limited viewpoint. Although the death of someone near to us and the suffering it causes is a monumental event, the death of every being is an unavoidable part of the greater scheme of our lives. Although today it is our wife who has died, tomorrow it may be our friend's wife or our neighbour's child. Although we are overcome by a state of disbelief and shock when our beloved dies, if we reflect deeply we will understand that everyone will at some point be affected by the death of someone close to them.

Normally we suffer greatly because we compare our circumstances to those of other people, who we think are much more fortunate than we are. The only difference, however, is the time at which misfortune befalls us, nothing else. If we reflect carefully upon this our sadness will diminish, as we can overcome our natural instinct to compare our plight with that of others. An even more powerful approach is to generate compassion. When we truly realise that we all endure the same struggles, as we all experience grief and loss at some time in our lives, then our own pain will diminish as we learn to view it from this much wider perspective.

Of course the death of someone close to us will affect us more than the death of a stranger, and it is only natural that we have such strong feelings for our own family. But ultimately we need to remember that death will affect every living being, and if we genuinely take this to heart it should not be so surprising. A story from the Buddha's life illustrates this point:[32]

> Once there was a young woman whose first born child fell ill and died when it was about one year old. Grief stricken, she begged anyone she met for a medicine that would restore the child to life, however, she was told that the only person who could perform this miracle was the Buddha. When she finally met the Buddha and told him her story, he told her to bring him back a mustard seed from any house in her village in which there had never been a death. It was not long, however, before she realised that the task the Buddha had set her could not be fulfilled. Every household had experienced death; not only once but some of them countless times. So finally the young woman said goodbye to her child for the last time and returned to the Buddha without the mustard seed. She had learnt her lesson. It wasn't only she that suffered at the hands of death, rather death happens to everyone—it is a natural part of life.

The Buddhist idea of reincarnation can also be helpful when dealing with loss and grief, as it reassures us that there is no such thing as *complete* death. By this I don't mean that our loved ones are always with us and watching over us, which is the impression we may get from some of the clairvoyants on television! This concept is limited, as it may give the impression that we are only ever connected to the same family or ancestors, rather than recognising the vast and ever-changing cycle of life that we are embedded in.

By saying there is no complete death, I am referring to the idea that each being goes through an endless series of lifetimes. Just as the physical continuum we call the universe continues on through time, so too does the mind-stream of all beings. Just as a flower goes through many 'incarnations', as it dies and its seeds give birth to a new flower, we can speak of our own mental continuum in a similar way. When we die, the gross physical body and gross mind cease to exist. However, a person's subtle mind, which contains the imprints of all their good and bad actions, continues on. I will discuss this further in the next chapter.

What this all means is that the time we have spent with our spouse is no more than a few moments in our unending journey. We have been like strangers who met in the pub or in a restaurant; we have spent some time together and have learnt from each other, but then we must part, as is natural. The mind of our loved one needs to continue on to its next lifetime, in the same way that we need to continue on with our own life.

I sometimes meet people who have lost a loved one many years before, and since that time they have been unable to stop thinking about this person, dwelling on how much they loved them and how dearly they miss them. Sometimes they think that by holding on so tightly to the memory of this person they are honouring their loved one and proving how much they loved them. This is not true, however, as by holding on so tightly to this memory they are hurting themselves, and this is not useful.

I am not saying we should forget our loved ones, but that we should instead remember and appreciate the wonderful time we spent together rather than holding on to our memories so tightly that we hurt ourselves. If a beautiful flower dies when winter comes, we accept this as being natural. It would be quite odd if someone cried and suffered because they couldn't accept this. If we reflect deeply, the death of any person is also just a natural part of life. Everyone's life will end sometime, and one day so must our life.

When I was in New Zealand I met a lady whose husband had just died. This lady, who was eighty-one years old, had been married to her husband for many years and had loved him dearly. Yet after his death she was still able to lead a happy existence. She could talk with enjoyment and gratitude of the times they had spent together, but she realised he needed to pass on to his next life, whereas she still had to live in this life. Interestingly, she also mentioned that her husband had been through quite a difficult time shortly before he died, though nevertheless he was able to find a deep sense of peace and wellbeing. Perhaps the courageous and accepting attitude of his wife helped him to do this.

FAILING HEALTH

Another loss that many people experience around this time is loss of good health. It is hard for some people to watch their health slip away, especially if they placed great value on their youth and vitality in the past. But declining health is an inevitable part of being alive. From the time we are born our physical bodies are losing health and vitality; and from the Buddhist perspective, we are gradually getting ready to have our bodies replaced again. Think about an old car, an old television or any material object; when it breaks down, at first we try to repair it. When it breaks down so much that it is beyond repair then we must get a new one. Similarly, when our body breaks down beyond repair, what we need is a new body!

Failing health also reminds us to practise gratitude. We can be grateful that we live in a wealthy country with good health facilities and people who have been trained to care for us. Remember there are many people in this world who die from a minor sickness or at a young age purely because there is no doctor or hospital to help them. My own father, for example, died at the age of forty-nine from a twisted bowel. There was only one doctor in our village, who misdiagnosed my father's condition and just gave him some medicines when what he really needed was surgery. I only learnt many years later that with a small operation his life could have easily been saved. I felt outraged and extremely disappointed for some years after, knowing that my father could have continued to live a rich and meaningful life as a Buddhist practitioner.

So how did I cope with these feelings? I had no choice, really. I realised it did not matter how angry or upset I felt over my father's death, as this would not bring him back to life. My negative emotions would not help him and they would only end up causing me harm. As a Buddhist, I also believed that it was my karma to lose my father at such a young age, in the same way that it was my father's karma to die at this time—this is really another way of saying that we should accept the things we cannot change. I also thought it was important to do what I could to honour my father's memory, and since he had always wished that I would become a monk, this is what I did. I had never been interested in being a monk beforehand, so it was his death that gave me the inspiration to change the direction of my life.

LOSS OF A JOB

The end of our working life can come through our own choice, such as when we retire, or through the will of others, if we are made redundant or find that our skills are no longer in demand. Most people think the first option would be wonderful, while the second is considered less pleasant. However, they really amount to the same thing and, either way, they cause people the same problems.

Many people dream of retiring for years, and then when this finally eventuates they feel a deep sense of loss and grief. Suddenly they find themselves bored, with nothing to do. I think this is largely because in the modern world our job is closely tied up with our identity and our self-esteem, and for many people it is also a status symbol.

But ask yourself, is it really that important? Reflect on this for a little while. Maybe being the big boss, amassing lots of money and having plenty of people under us makes us feel good about ourselves. However, this does not mean we are a good person; rather, it is likely to be rooted in attachment to the pleasurable feeling of power and self-importance! By feeding these emotions we are chaining ourselves to them, leading us to suffer when our conditions change, as they inevitably will. If we did not cling so much to these emotions it is likely that far less sorrow would come our way.

Often people find that they have too much free time when they stop working. What many people may not realise, however, is that this free time can give us a precious opportunity to develop ourselves and discover our inner nature, making an effort to cultivate all the good qualities we have mentioned. Often people die at a young age, during a time when they were busy juggling many things such as establishing a career or raising children. We are fortunate enough to now have the time and opportunity, without so many external things to distract us, to focus more on our inner life. We will always have plenty to do each day if we focus on our mind and inner development.[33] At first we may need to devote considerable time and effort to this task, but soon it will become much more fun than watching television or playing bingo!

So how can we develop these inner qualities? There are many different ways to achieve this through helping others, for example by teaching a language to refugees, helping out in a soup kitchen or volunteering as a telephone counsellor. Becoming involved in these kinds of activities stops us from feeling as though we have too much spare time, and by helping others we will experience more and more happiness in our lives.

An active, charitable life can also be backed up by a regular commitment to 'train the mind in wisdom', as this can make your ability to help others even more effective. You could read and contemplate books on psychology, religion or philosophy, and apply the ideas you learn to your own life, or discuss these ideas with others. Then, in addition to the joys of an altruistic life, you will discover the joy of having a sharp, wise mind. Finally, as scientists now believe that even older people can generate new brain cells[34] through training the mind, a regular commitment to study or contemplation can be a powerful way to slow down the age-related memory impairment which sadly afflicts so many of the elderly.

If we are concerned that we are not clever enough to spend hours reading books trying to increase our wisdom, it is helpful to know there is a big difference between being wise and being intelligent. A wise person may not necessarily have a good education or an important job; instead, they may just have an innate practical understanding of what is important in life, and it is likely they are just naturally a kind person. There are many stories in Tibet of people who led an extremely simple life and did not have any formal education whatsoever, but were always known for their kindness and wisdom.

How can we be like these people? The key is to continually think about and wish that all others will be happy and free from suffering, in the same way that a good mother wants nothing but the best for her child. If we can always have a warm heart, thinking of every individual as our dearest child while walking, talking, sleeping, eating, or doing any kind of activity, then over time we will forget our own self-interest and will naturally feel happier and wiser. Even if we are too tired or too unwell to actually help others, the most important thing is that we train our mind to think in a thoughtful and kind way. I have no doubt that we will then gradually become kinder, wiser and happier people.

FINANCES

By this age, most people's focus has naturally drifted away from making money. This is a good thing for our happiness! I still want to mention money, however, as the way we use our money and possessions at this age is still important, and unfortunately there are still many traps we can fall into. One of these traps is being miserly. Some people do not want to spend money on anyone except themselves, while others are so miserly that they will not even spend money on themselves. How senseless never to spend anything after a life of hard work!

If we have saved up a reasonable amount of money, how should we then spend it? By this stage we will probably have learnt from experience that money is unlikely to buy us happiness, though it can certainly be of great benefit if we use it wisely. Just say we have $5,000 to spend. We could choose to go for a holiday on a tropical island or we could donate this money to a poor family and perhaps save the life of someone who needs an operation. We often spend money on an expensive holiday or a new car because we want a change, feeling dissatisfied or bored with our current situation. This might seem very appealing at the time but it will not lead to lasting happiness. Helping another living being by being generous, in contrast, will give us an immediate sense of wellbeing and will also plant a seed for future happiness in our mind.

This does not mean, however, that we should give all our money away, leaving almost nothing for ourselves and then going into debt to buy gifts for others. One of my friends informed me that many people in Australia spend large amounts of money on gifts for their family and friends at Christmas, at times much more than they can really afford. Their motivation may be good but this type of kindness is often impractical and lacking in wisdom, especially if they are struggling to make ends meet. Being in debt can greatly restrict our freedom, yet this form of suffering can usually be prevented if we are wise about how we spend.

While it is important to be generous and help others, it is also crucial to be honest about our situation and try to see clearly how much we can afford. We should ask ourselves how we can use our wealth most effectively, taking all circumstances into account. This is what I mean by wisdom. Also remember that being generous doesn't just mean giving material gifts. The gift of our time, love and care, for example by helping out with the cooking or cleaning on Christmas day, is just as important and just as appreciated by those around us.

LONELINESS AND INTOLERANCE

Many people are worried or even afraid that they will become lonely as they get older. There are several practical things we can do to avoid loneliness. If we are able, we can become involved with people in our community who need help. We may start teaching a language to migrants, volunteer at a school, or find out how we can use our skills and expertise to assist volunteer organisations like the Red Cross, or perhaps our local church or temple.

If we are not in good shape physically but our mind is strong, then study and spiritual practice can be a very rewarding way to spend our time. As hermits who go on long retreats will testify, we can feel incredibly close to others if we meditate on compassion, and we can also develop good inner focus. Although we may be alone, this does not mean we have to feel lonely.

Becoming involved with community or religious groups is a good way to meet new people and we will become friends with many of them. Some of them, however, may push our buttons. I mention this in order to bring up the issue of intolerance, which I feel is a big reason why people are often lonely in the West. In western culture, many people seem to value their 'personal space' and 'personal freedom' highly, only wanting to associate with people who have similar ideas and compatible personalities; however, this inevitably creates barriers.

The first point I wish to make is that no particular custom or personality type is better than another. This is just habitual thinking on our part, and we need to learn to practise tolerance towards everyone, whether we like them straight away or find them irritating. It is very common to meet someone and feel a strong initial aversion to them, but then over time come to like and appreciate them. This does not mean that the person has changed their inherent nature, rather it means that *our* mind has transformed its perception of them.

Another common way that intolerance becomes a problem is when we create physical or emotional barriers around ourselves. By this I mean we may inadvertently create barriers by holding tightly to the idea that some space or some time is for us alone. We may think, for example, that someone opening our door or someone visiting us without any notice is an intrusion into our personal space. How different this is from Tibet! When I was living in monasteries in Tibet, it would not matter if I was trying to study, trying to dress or even trying to wash, the other monks would often make themselves at home in my room and go through my possessions. I didn't feel annoyed or irritated, as this was a normal part of the culture. However, having lived in the West for a few years, if someone now visits me without notice or opens my door, I do feel as though this is not so appropriate.

Unfortunately, our concept of personal space often creates distance between people, and if we are distant we are more likely to become lonely. If we lived in a completely open environment with no personal boundaries, we might easily get on each other's nerves. On the other hand, letting go of the attitude that we 'need' personal space can lead to closeness and tolerance of each other. I must confess I didn't really know what loneliness was until I came to the West—I thought loneliness was the same as boredom! Now that I am aware of how big a problem it is, I feel it is especially important to help people see the disadvantages of being attached to their personal space.

At this point I would like to use a personal example to illustrate a point about tolerance. In one monastery where I used to live there was a monk with a very short temper who would quickly become angry whenever other monks interrupted or joked around with him. The other monks would then purposely set out to annoy him again and again, as it was so easy to make him angry. This may sound cruel, but over time his temperament and self-control became much better, since he realised that his anger achieved nothing and he was happier when he practised tolerance towards others.

Tolerance does not just extend towards other people. We have very little control over what happens in our lives, so we will inevitably face many external events that we would rather not face. If we are intolerant we will find it difficult to attain peace, as these events will lead to anger and distress, eating away at our good will.

Alternatively, we can use every situation that frustrates us and every person we find annoying as an opportunity to practise tolerance. We can do this every single day until it becomes a habit. First familiarise yourself with the advantages of acting in this way and the disadvantages of not doing so, and then, as a ritual, be mindful of practising tolerance all the time. You will be rewarded with more loving relationships and a mind as peaceful as a cloudless blue sky.

GRATITUDE

Gratitude is another positive mental quality we can practise every single day. There is a very good reason to do this, as feeling grateful towards others makes us feel happier ourselves. This is not only a Buddhist belief—psychological studies have also found gratitude to be a contributing factor to human happiness.[35]

Sometimes when I mention this to people they respond that they are too unhappy to feel grateful. They tell me they are lonely, they have little money or they do not have a good relationship with their children, and therefore they have nothing for which to be grateful. This is never true, as there is always something to be grateful for if we are just able to recognise it. For example, when I came to Australia it was the first time I had a telephone in my house. What a wonderful invention! I was suddenly able to speak with people on the other side of the world from my own home. How grateful I was to the person who had invented this! Now I feel the same way about the internet, about flying in an aeroplane, and even about sticky tape when I need to stick something to my wall. Not to mention the many people who help put food on my table each day and those who offer the gift of their friendship.

Some people may not accept this reasoning and think to themselves, 'I still have to pay for many of these things so why should I feel grateful?' However, someone still had to design and build the aeroplane, the telephone and the sticky tape for me to be able to use them. If I was the richest man in the world but nobody had invented the telephone, then I would not be able to talk to people on a different continent! Furthermore, we should remember that there are many things to be grateful for which no amount of money can buy, such as the kindness of family and friends or the natural beauty of the world around us.

By feeling gratitude for things in our daily lives we are able to cultivate happiness within ourselves. This makes us mentally stronger and allows us to cope better with many of the problems of life, including ageing, loss and eventually death. It is important to remember, however, that there are two sides to gratitude. It is wonderful if we can feel grateful for everything and everyone around us; however, we must guard ourselves against becoming attached to these things. If this happens we will try to hold onto them and inevitably suffer when they are taken away. It is difficult to really understand how we can appreciate things without being attached to them, yet this is a crucial skill if we wish to live a happy and meaningful life.

Remember that everything has good points and bad points, including the telephone, the aeroplane and the sticky tape. Our phone bills might be expensive, our flight may be delayed, and we may not be able to find the end of the sticky tape! But if we don't feel grateful for what we have, we are training our minds to dwell on the negative points and are sure to end up dissatisfied. We will never truly be happy, as it is impossible to have everything we wish for all of the time. In essence, although the world is filled with much suffering, there are also many wonders. Cultivating gratitude does not mean making ourselves see the world through rose coloured glasses, but rather learning to appreciate these many wonders for what they are.

EXERCISE — REFLECTING ON IMPERMANENCE

Bring to mind some of the losses and changes you have witnessed by this time in your life, and contemplate the following thoughts:

- *Whatever is born will get old and die.*
- *What has been gathered will be dispersed.*
- *What has been accumulated will be exhausted.*
- *What has been built up will collapse.*

In the same way, friendship and enmity, fortune and sorrow, all the thoughts that run through our mind—everything is always changing.

Remind yourself that impermanence is simply the truth of how life is, and therefore the only thing we really have is now, the present.

How could this understanding help you cope with the loss of a loved one?

How could it change your perspective on the different types of losses that we face—the loss of dear ones, the loss of a job, or the loss of anything we hold dear?

It may also help to remember that changes do not necessarily lead to misfortune—sometimes they may benefit you greatly, even though this may not be obvious at first.

Reflecting on all these questions, sit with your back straight, feel your body relax and take a few big, gentle breaths. What lessons does the truth of impermanence hold for you?

Preparing for Departure from this Life

The sixth stage of life is the last and most vital opportunity for self-realisation. I will talk more directly about spirituality in this chapter because at this age spiritual practice is far more important for most people than ever before. It doesn't matter what has happened in our past. There is no point having regrets about how we have lived our life up until this point—we must remember we still have the opportunity and ability to work on our mind and attain happiness. Most importantly, at this stage in life, without exception, everyone has the opportunity to prepare for a peaceful death and use this crucial time as an opportunity for self-realisation.

As my training is in Buddhism, I will speak mostly from a Buddhist point of view. In western culture, however, there are two other major viewpoints which in many ways are equally valid—the theistic point of view, coming mainly from the Christian, Jewish and Islamic traditions, and the secular point of view, which embraces science and usually holds an atheistic or agnostic outlook.

From the theistic point of view, we can prepare for death by cultivating qualities of love and compassion, so we can become 'close to God'. We are also encouraged to make a sincere heartfelt confession of all our negative actions, knowing that it is never too late to ask for forgiveness and find true peace if we are genuine. We can accept hardships and suffering as the 'will of God', and this allows us to find a state of inner peace, calm and confidence. There is also an understanding that a good person will go to heaven as a result of his or her good deeds and faith.

From a secular point of view, there are many people who don't have any particular expectations about life after death. This can be a very useful attitude, as it can stop us from holding onto ideas and concepts which might prove unhelpful, leading to less fear and more inner calm. No matter what our beliefs, however, we will have discovered through life experience that kindness, compassion and a good heart are essential qualities which nourish every aspect of our life. Negative attitudes, on the other hand, only cause harm for ourselves and others. Therefore it makes sense to focus on these positive qualities when we are close to death, and try our best to let go of all our negativity. For those who have a strong conviction that we no longer exist after we die, in some ways this too can be a useful attitude, as it can help us realise how incredibly precious this life is and inspire us to make the most of it.

Now I shall talk about some concepts from the Buddhist point of view, which I feel can be helpful for everyone, regardless of their religious or cultural background. My hope is that you will see how these principles relate to your own belief system, and then apply them to your own life.

KARMA

What goes around, comes around.
— *Traditional proverb* —

❧

With our thoughts we make the world.
— *Buddha* —

❧

As ye sow, so shall ye reap.

— *Jesus Christ* —

Most people, Buddhist and non-Buddhist alike, are already familiar with the concept of karma. However, to make sure we understand it clearly, I would like to use a couple of analogies.

Just imagine we have a tub filled with clear water and then we put some dirt or some colouring dye into it. The water will become clouded. In the same way, our mind is like that clear water, and any action or thought that we have will be imprinted in our mind-stream. We must understand that whatever we think, say or do depends on the mind, as our actions start with the mind and finish with the mind. The mind is therefore like a king, and the body and speech are like its servants, carrying out whatever the mind instructs. Thus, whatever we do is imprinted in the mind. According to Buddhism, mind and speech depend on the physical body and are therefore temporary and destructible, whereas the subtle mind does not depend on physical matter and therefore endures after we die. For this reason, we have the idea of continuous cycles of life, with the imprints in the mind carrying on from one lifetime to the next.

Another analogy is a bank. When we earn money through working hard we put this into a bank, and then later, when we need to use this money, it is there waiting for us. Similarly, when we have a positive thought or commit a positive action, we accrue merit for our future; however, when we think or act in a negative way, we take away from this merit, and if we take away a substantial amount we will eventually have to pay back the debt.

Karma is a fundamental concept in Buddhism,[36] although even if we do not have any spiritual beliefs it still applies to us. If we do something unkind or unthoughtful towards a person, this will result in two unpleasant consequences. First of all, that person will dislike us, and secondly, we will feel regret. We may not notice this at first, but underneath we will always have some regret in our heart, which will come to the surface eventually. On the other hand, as psychological studies now show, if we are kind to someone we will feel happier in ourselves, and the other person is also more likely to be kind to us in return.[37] The only real difference between these simple facts and what Buddhists believe is the idea that we carry the karma we have accrued in this life into our next life.

How are our future lives created by our karma? If we are always very generous, we will firstly notice that the people around us are generous towards us in return. We may even notice that many people we have never met are also generous to us, so financial and other forms of success are easy to come by. Most of us would probably call this good luck, but Buddhists would say that these favourable external conditions are actually the result of our previous good actions, or karma, in this lifetime or in previous lifetimes. On the other hand, if we have poor external conditions at the present, this is because of bad karma we are working off. This is based on the idea that everything is interdependent and therefore nothing is random, even what we normally think of as good or bad 'luck'.

Therefore we should not feel disheartened if our conditions are bad, nor should we feel proud if our conditions are fortunate. The person who is living the 'good life' is in fact using up good karma from his or her karma bank, while the person who is experiencing hardship is using up or 'purifying' bad karma. They both, however, have the opportunity to create good conditions for themselves in their current and future lifetimes by performing good actions.

SUFFERING AND PURIFICATION

Suffering is closely linked to karma for Buddhists. Buddha stated that suffering is the first truth in life, that if we are to live we are to suffer.[38] We already know this in our lives because things inevitably go wrong—we experience heartbreak and we lose people and things that we care about. So if we can't avoid the external events which cause suffering, then what can we do to overcome it? The answer is that we need to understand that the root causes of suffering are found in our previous negative emotions and negative actions. Through being mindful of this truth, we can learn to generate wholesome states of mind and learn to observe, accept and let go of the thoughts and emotions that are racing through our minds, instead of holding onto them tightly. Through this process we can reduce our current level of suffering and gradually, step by step, remove suffering altogether.

The first thing we must understand is that suffering is created by ourselves, by our own minds and no-one else. The external conditions that we think bring suffering are in fact secondary conditions, and these are the result of karma. This does not mean we should blame ourselves for our external conditions—blame is not important or helpful. Rather, we must understand the reasons for our external conditions and then address them.

So if present as well as future suffering is a consequence of negative karma, what can we do about it? Are we condemned to live out the consequences of our past actions, or can we change this situation?

Thankfully, it is possible to purify our past karma, as long as we are genuine about this. This can prevent future suffering and can also lessen our experience of suffering during the dying process. To wash something dirty we need soap and water. When we wash away negative karma, we need four conditions:

1. Regret

Heartfelt acceptance needs to be generated for whatever conflicts or issues have troubled you throughout your life, along with regret for whatever wrong you may have committed. This includes everything you don't remember from this lifetime, and perhaps also things from previous lifetimes. The ability to remember everything, however, is not as important as the strength and genuineness of the feeling you generate. You can think, 'Here I am, this is me. I have nothing to hide; I accept myself completely and I honestly acknowledge all my flaws'. Remember not to confuse regret with guilt or unhealthy shame, as the idea is to openly state your negative tendencies without being self-critical. You are giving yourself permission to accept every part of who you are as a human being and then to let go of everything which is weighing you down.

2. Applying the Antidote

This means you should strive hard to perform good actions and cultivate wholesome states of mind, as this is part of the purification process. Generate compassion towards others and ask for forgiveness in whatever way is meaningful to you, asking or praying for help to wash away your negative karma. Many people find it helpful to think in terms of surrendering to a 'higher power', whether it be God, Buddha or the common human potential for goodness. Viewing things from this perspective, you may find you are able to forgive those against whom you have had a grudge, speak openly to those who have grown distant, or even resolve longstanding conflicts. The most important result of this practice, however, is the transformation of your own state of mind.

3. Resolution

This means you should be genuinely determined not to repeat the same actions or habits which have caused you to make negative karma or live in a state of emotional conflict. The importance of this cannot be overstated. Your determination should be such that even if your life was at stake you would refuse to commit this action or think this way again. It is said that a strong and sincere resolution can be powerful enough to purify many lifetimes worth of negative karma. This does not depend on the amount of time you spend thinking in this way, but rather on the genuineness and strength of your commitment.

4. Intensity

Finally, you need to have a high degree of focus, thinking intensely of all the negative actions you have ever committed and truly acknowledging all the things you want to change. You can fervently pray that all this be washed away. There are thousands of formal prayers in Buddhism, and also many in Christianity and other religions, but if you don't know any formal prayers you can just say whatever comes from the heart. It doesn't really matter what you say, as long as it is genuine and sincere. It can then be very powerful.

The suffering experienced when dying can be great. A person's mental suffering, however, is often much greater than his or her physical suffering. By learning how to purify negative karma, the experience of mental suffering can be greatly reduced. Even the physical suffering, although we still go through it, will not burden us nearly as much as it once would have. We may still experience suffering, but it will not overwhelm us.

Western psychology has identified the various stages we go through after finding out we have a terminal illness or indeed are confronted with any piece of unexpected bad news.[39] These include: denial that anything is wrong in the first place, anger or frustration that things aren't going our way, and then depression and loss of confidence when we see we are caught in something we have no control over. Finally, although not all people reach this stage, we can arrive at a state of peaceful and genuine acceptance, learning to let go of all the struggles we have been going through and view life with a renewed sense of depth and wisdom. If we understand the truth of suffering and work hard to purify our karma, we can come to this stage of peace and acceptance much sooner.

A final point is that if we are ill and tired, it is important to accept the suffering that comes with this rather than trying to fight against it or forcing ourselves to engage with the outside world. Accepting the suffering also frees us from feeling guilty that we can no longer live up to previous commitments and responsibilities, which only adds unnecessary pain to the suffering we are already going through. Modern culture is so focused on getting ahead and keeping busy that it is often difficult to really give ourselves permission to listen to our bodies and rest when we need to. This is true for people at any stage of life, but especially towards the end of life when many of us are forced to 'slow down' for the first time.

COMPASSION

If someone is unhappy and has a problem, I often suggest that they practise compassion. They may respond, 'I am so unhappy myself, how can I possibly have compassion for others?' This way of thinking seems to suggest that compassion equates to sympathy or feeling sorry for others, and that we will suffer more if we take on their burdens. However, suffering usually comes when we ignore the feelings of others and are caught up in our own pride and vanity. Therefore, generating true compassion towards others can be a very effective way to reduce our own suffering.

Although it can be incredibly beneficial to practise compassion, many people have a limited idea of what compassion actually is, thinking it means feeling sorry for others while we are left with a feeling of discomfort. The logical conclusion may well be, 'Feeling compassion for another makes me suffer and therefore I shouldn't think about the suffering of another'. This is a very limited way of thinking, as genuine compassion always goes hand in hand with wisdom and should therefore never make us suffer or become weak. Why is this? Genuine compassion means we understand the causes of suffering and how each living being, starting with ourselves, has the potential to overcome suffering. By then mentally taking the suffering of others upon ourselves, we can develop a strong and courageous mind which actually protects us from experiencing suffering!

Let me give an example of how we can combine compassion with wisdom. If someone shoots a person or steals his possessions, then normally it is easy to feel compassion for the one who has lost money or even their life, and to be angry with the person who has committed the crime, but by combining compassion with wisdom, we realise how both are objects of compassion. Firstly, the person who lost money suffers as a result of many factors, including their previous negative karma, while the one who has committed the crime does so under the control of afflictive emotions, and is creating new suffering for himself in the future as a consequence of his action (which may even increase in future lifetimes). It is on this basis that compassion can be extended equally to all living beings, friends and enemies alike.

This type of compassion not only seeks to understand the suffering of others, but also makes us poised to act in order to alleviate their suffering. It is wonderful if we are in a position to help others, yet even if we cannot help, we should remember that having compassion will definitely help us. To understand the suffering of others is to reduce our own suffering, as we realise we are all going through similar struggles and it no longer makes sense to focus on our own problems. Like ripples that spread out when a stone is thrown into a pond, an attitude of compassion may also help those with whom we interact, such as friends and family. This can be a catalyst for building peace between ourselves and others, and also among other people who see our example. Who knows how far the ripples of our compassion will spread?

OVERCOMING FEAR OF DYING

Dying is just like changing clothes
— His Holiness the Dalai Lama —

⌒

In general, people tend to avoid thinking about death, but sooner or later we must realise it is inevitable. As we grow older we may therefore have an increased fear of death, a fear which is largely based on three main factors. Firstly there is the dread of losing loved ones and possessions, along with the fear of annihilation. Then there is the fear of the physical pain of dying. Finally, we have to confront the fear of facing the consequences of misdeeds we may have committed, often accompanied by a profound sense of regret. All of these fears, however, can be overcome if we know how.

From a Buddhist point of view, attachment is the source of suffering and should therefore be abandoned. If we are attached to our loved ones, the fear we have of losing them may cause us significant distress. To alleviate this fear, it is very helpful to think of everyone we are associated with in this life, even those closest to us, as though they are like people we pass in the street or figures that appear in a dream. In the greater scheme of things, they are simply passing acquaintances.

This does not mean, however, that we will never meet our loved ones again. Indeed, if we let go of our attachment, there is actually a greater chance that we will meet them again in a favourable situation. This is because the positive interactions we have had with them, based on kindness and generosity, are sure to draw us together again when the conditions are right. Although we do have to say good-bye to all our loved ones, we can actually look forward to death if we view it as a new beginning waiting to unfold and are able to lessen our attachment to our old life.

We may also have a deep-seated fear of physical pain. In response to this, it can help to be aware that not everybody experiences a painful death. Many people in fact die painlessly and with a truly peaceful mind. If we do experience pain, however, it is helpful to generate a strong mind and an attitude which bravely accepts the pain, instead of viewing it with fear or aversion. More importantly, we should be aware that the pain we experience can be a way of purifying enormous amounts of negative karma, especially if we are able to keep a virtuous state of mind. When we are sick the experience of pain is often a sign that our body is healing. It is helpful to think in the same way when our bodies are going through the transition to a new birth.

Secondly, it is crucial that the mind is not occupied only by the pain or by grasping onto it. Even when we experience it, how well we cope depends on how much we can let go of our reaction to the sensation of pain, which is sometimes overwhelming. It is thus helpful to learn how to just 'watch' the pain or let it fade into the background, or see it as just sensation, filling our mind with strong, virtuous thoughts such as the inspiration of God or whatever represents our deepest truth.

To cope with feelings of regret, we must first understand that it is good to feel a sense of regret for any wrong actions we may have committed. We must remember that any negative actions and their results are only temporary and therefore should not define who we are. Instead, our true nature is fundamentally pure and unpolluted by afflictive emotions, just like a clear sky untainted by clouds. The greater our feeling of genuine regret for all our wrong actions, the greater our power to purify ourselves using the four conditions mentioned previously—regret, applying an antidote, resolution and intensity. Remember, genuine regret does not mean we should dwell in feelings of guilt and do nothing. Instead, it should motivate us to truly accept who we are and what has happened during our lives, and do our best to clear away unwholesome states of mind and cultivate wholesome mental qualities.

It can also be very helpful to understand what happens when we die.

Much of this knowledge comes from the tantric practices of Tibetan Buddhism, by which great practitioners would train themselves to practice consciously passing through the experience of death while still alive. We are very fortunate that such knowledge is now widely available, as it can help us to know exactly what to expect during the dying process and assist us to overcome the fear of annihilation.

Death is actually a process we experience every day when we fall asleep. When we fall asleep, the gross mind, which consists of our ordinary thoughts and emotions, dissolves into the subtle mind, and we can experience feelings such as bliss and clarity when this takes place. When we die, the subtle mind becomes even more subtle and the energies of the physical body dissolve one by one into the four elements: earth, water, fire and wind. This is why when we die we first feel extremely heavy, as though we are drowning, as the earth element is gradually dissolving into the water element. Next we feel extremely dehydrated, as the water element dissolves, and then our body becomes cold with the dissolution of the fire element. Finally, we find it hard to move, and gradually our breathing stops as the wind element dissolves.

There are many more details to this process of dissolution,[40] and these can be found in specific books devoted to the subject. It is important to know, however, that the process is not complete when breathing ceases. Although the breath and heartbeat have both ceased and the person is normally considered dead, the mental processes of dying are continuing, and therefore it is advisable not to move them for some time or distract them with noise. Such interruptions might actually disturb the dying person's subtle mind while the final phases of dissolution are taking place, leading to mental unrest during certain stages.

In Tibet, there are many cases of spiritual practitioners who have shown complete mastery over the dying process, and often their bodies are still warm, especially over the heart centre, many days after respiration has ceased. To give an example, my own teacher Lama

Lobsang Trinley and his spiritual brother Lama Rinpal were both able to announce their time of death and passed away in deep meditative absorption without sickness. The great 16th Karmapa was always joyful throughout his final illness, and many days after his death his heart was found to still be warm,[41] baffling western doctors and scientists. This shows that there can still be a connection between the mind and the body long after we normally think a person has 'died'.

For most people, however, while we are separating from our present body our subtle mind slowly becomes more gross and we are propelled towards a new rebirth. This is elaborated upon in the 'bardo teachings', with the term bardo describing an intermediate state or process between one life and the next. In this state our conscious awareness re-emerges with the capacity to sense, feel and recognise things once again, but without the support of a physical body. After a transition period which is said to last about seven weeks, this conscious awareness generally takes rebirth once again in a new body.[42]

We all wish for a peaceful death, but this depends on how we have lived our life. It is important to live a peaceful life and strive hard to develop good mental qualities such as loving kindness, compassion, forgiveness and tolerance. As we approach death it is extremely important to focus on developing these qualities, since this is a very powerful time and we have a great opportunity to guarantee ourselves a peaceful death and an auspicious rebirth.

PRACTICES FOR THE MOMENT OF DEATH

There are two important spiritual practices we can undertake to help us achieve a peaceful death. The first is a more extensive practice of purification that we can perform either some time before death or at the time of death, if we have the energy. The second practice is a very special and practical method to help us achieve rebirth in a pure realm or heaven. Such a realm reflects the qualities of enlightened beings and is free from suffering, as there is no chance for afflictive mental states to arise, and the beings who dwell there spontaneously possess wholesome states of mind and divine perception.

Both of these practices, however, rely on our ability to develop a calm and settled mind. It is therefore crucial to first learn the basics of meditation practice. I will therefore give a brief overview of how to meditate before describing these important practices.

Learning to Meditate

Unfortunately, our minds are usually so scattered that it is difficult to focus on an object without losing concentration. It is therefore crucial to learn a method or routine to mindfully bring the mind and body to a relaxed, calm and alert state whenever we choose.[43] This begins by knowing the correct meditation postures.

The Four Meditation Postures

One can meditate while sitting, lying down, walking or standing—and each of these postures can be used formally or informally.

For sitting, you should use a comfortable straight-backed padded chair or a meditation stool or cushion. The hands rest together either in the lap or on the thighs, while the back is held erect with the chin slightly tucked in. The jaw, tongue, shoulders and abdomen are all relaxed, with the eyes either closed or half-open, gently gazing downwards. Placing the tongue behind the top teeth can make the mind more alert, while keeping it behind the bottom teeth can help you achieve a more relaxed and calm state.

For lying down, you can either lie on your back with your arms by your side and hands open, or on the right side with your right hand underneath your face, legs together with the knees slightly bent and your left arm down the left side of your body. For walking and standing, you should hold your hands, right in left, in front of your body, letting your arms hang naturally and being sure to have an upright but relaxed posture.

The Basic Meditation Method

All types of meditation follow the same basic method, and this begins by consciously relaxing the body. A good way to achieve this is to do some gentle 'loosening exercises' prior to medi-tating, such as shaking or massaging different parts of your body or performing gentle yoga stretches. You should then consciously drop all concerns about the past and future, resolving to become someone with 'no history' while you are meditating. Then focus your mind on aware-ness of the present moment, including your breath, the physical presence of your body, the feelings in your body, the sounds around you and the state of your mind, noticing how all these things arise and pass away.

Once your mindfulness is well established, you can continue to focus on the present moment, anchored by the awareness of breathing through your entire body (and knowing whether you are breathing a long breath or a short breath). Alternatively, you can shift your awareness towards a specific meditation object such as a visualisa-tion, a sound, contemplation of a topic such as loving kindness or pure awareness of the breath at your heart or the tip of your nose.

It is inevitable that thoughts will arise, and you should just watch or notice these with the 'awareness aspect' of your mind without grasping at them, and then gently return to the meditation object. Sounds and other sensations will still be there in the background; part of your mind will be aware of these sensations, yet they do not have to disturb your mindfulness if you can simply watch them without reacting. By practising in this way you should eventually arrive at a state where the body is relaxed, the emotions are calm and the mind is clear.

At first short, frequent sessions are the best way to develop a calm and balanced state of mind. That way, the practice will be enjoyable and interesting and you will be sure to notice a difference after doing it for some time. A calm state of mind will allow you to really feel the effect of the two practices that follow and gain real insight into their true meaning.

Purification Practice

The most crucial task in preparing for death is to purify our negative karma. This requires the four conditions I previously discussed: regret, applying the antidote, resolution and intensity. We can make this practice even more powerful with a particular visualisation which Buddhists call Vajrasattva.[44] Vajrasattva is a brilliant white deity who embodies purity, compassion and the power to heal. For those with different spiritual inclinations, it is important to perform this practice with the support of whatever represents this truth for you. For example, you may choose to visualise Jesus, a loving presence in the form of radiant white light, or perhaps an image from nature such as the sun shining through a shower of light-filled rain.

First adopt one of the meditation postures described above, whichever one is most comfortable for you. Recall anything you have done wrong in this life and openly acknowledge this, together with all the pain you have been holding onto, for whatever reason. You may also acknowledge that you have committed many negative acts over numerous lifetimes. Visualise the form of Vajrasattva (or whatever embodies this truth for you) above your head, white in colour like the moon yet translucent, adorned with jewels and seated cross-legged on a white lotus flower. Ask with heartfelt honesty, 'Compassionate one, please purify all my negative karma'.

You then visualise the divine milk-like nectar of bliss, compassion and forgiveness flowing from Vajrasattva's heart and soaking into every pore in your skin and every cell of your body, washing away all your negative karma and harmful emotions. All the dirt is washed away and leaves from the lower part of your body in the form of black smoke, ink or dirty blood, disappearing under the ground. Slowly the divine nectar

Vajrasattva, the embodiment of purity
in the Tibetan Buddhist tradition.

then fills your body, which becomes like a crystal, as if you have poured milk into a glass. This is not just a visualisation but something you can really feel throughout your entire body.

If you find this visualisation challenging, an alternative form of the practice is to visualise the warmth of the sun gradually filling your body, followed by a gentle shower of light-filled rain, washing over your skin and then through all of your muscles, bones and internal organs. It is best to adopt a form of the practice which best evokes for you a feeling of calm, bliss and radiance throughout your body.

Every day, as often as you can, you should continue with this visualisation and become confident that you have purified your negative karma and harmful emotions. Eventually, when you have purified your karma sufficiently, you will no longer have a fear of death or be plagued by regrets, leading the way to a peaceful death and a precious rebirth.

You can tell the practice is working when you can feel the white, radiant blissful nectar fill your entire body, and you will feel a conviction that you are purified, as though a large weight has been removed from your shoulders.

Why Vajrasattva? In the Buddhist tradition, it is said that there was once a saint known as Vajrasattva who attained enlightenment with the aspiration of purifying other people's negative karma, which is similar to Christ dying on the cross to purify the sins of the world. Therefore, praying with the support of Vajrasattva, or Jesus if you are Christian, can be especially powerful.

Practice to be Reborn Free from Suffering

If we have the desire to be reborn beautiful, wealthy or powerful, this is certainly achievable if we are equipped with the method to purify our negative karma and the aspiration to be reborn in this way. However, being reborn as someone beautiful, wealthy or powerful does not guarantee we will be free from suffering in our future lives.

If we really wish to be free from suffering, it is best to aspire towards rebirth in a pure land or heavenly realm. There is an entire school of Buddhism ('Pure Land Buddhism') which emphasises training the mind with this aspiration, so that as we approach the moment of death we can be confident and familiar with the transition to rebirth in the pure realm called Sukhavati. Although these teachings originate from Buddhist scripture and date back many centuries, they are not outdated and neither are they just dogma. Rather, they have been confirmed time and time again by the direct experience of highly realised practitioners, even nowadays, and on many occasions the deaths of these practitioners have been accompanied by miraculous signs. Indeed I have personally witnessed this in Tibet many times. To give an example, on one occasion a woman in my village who was dying from throat cancer told me she had been afraid of death for a few weeks, until one day she saw a vision of the red Buddha Amitabha before her—from that time she completely

Buddha Amitabha

lost all fear of dying and felt joyful and comfortable, with no concern whatsoever for physical pain.

By diligently practising the meditation to familiarise ourselves with the heaven of Sukhavati, we will create the conditions for a fearless, peaceful and joyful death, confident that we will have a wonderful new rebirth. Please understand that this practice is not just for Buddhists. If you have strong faith in God or a great being like Jesus, this is Sukhavati for you and therefore the practice will still be effective for you.

Why is Sukhavati so special? Just as Vajrasattva dedicated his enlightenment to purifying our negative karma, it is said that a bodhisattva, or great being, known as Amitabha once aspired to free people from suffering at the moment of death and, through his enlightenment, created the heaven of Sukhavati. This does not mean he built this place; rather, he dedicated oceans of positive karma so that a pure realm would manifest, in which people would be reborn if their aspirations were truly genuine.

If we are reborn in a pure realm then we are innately perfect. This means we naturally possess supreme mental qualities, much superior in fact to the qualities I have described in this book. In particular, we have devotion, diligence, supreme memory and clairvoyance, concentration, compassion and wisdom. We are born this way, a physically and mentally perfect being with a divine air. Although we may still have certain propensities, there is no opportunity for negative emotions or bad habits to take us over because the external conditions are blessed by Amitabha's divine power. For example, there is no-one who will provoke arguments and no environmental conditions that lead to any type of decay, suffering or negative emotions. Therefore, all our karma will naturally be purified and we will never again be born in an impure realm unless by our own choice. We will truly be free.

How do we reach Amitabha's pure realm? The teachings speak of four conditions, which are very simple and effective. Keep in mind that this is an extraordinarily precious and powerful practice. It is extremely rare to come across this teaching and have the good fortune to practise it.

1. Genuine Aspiration

You have to have a truly genuine intention and desire to be reborn in Sukhavati. Normally we think of desire as an obstacle to a peaceful death; however, here we have a unique chance to use this emotion to aspire to be reborn in Sukhavati. As human beings we are usually controlled by desire, but now we have a chance to direct it so we can reach Amitabha's pure realm.

2. Familiarisation

You need to be familiar with the pure realm, and especially the form of Amitabha, which is like a gateway to entering Sukhavati. Therefore, it is suggested that you do a visualisation practice, either of the Buddha Amitabha or any divine image you feel a heart connection with, adopting one of the formal meditation postures described above.

Amitabha is traditionally depicted as ruby red in colour, like a ruby mountain shining in the light of a thousand suns. He is wearing the simple robes of a monk, sitting cross-legged with hands in the meditation position (right hand over left, resting in the lap). The red colour symbolises human desire, with Buddha Amitabha manifesting to liberate us through desire. Traditionally his form is visualised above the crown of our head or in front of us at the level of our forehead, facing us. Normally the image is much bigger than the size of a human being, even as big as a mountain, though it can be any size you are comfortable with. You can then imagine immeasurable loving kindness extending from Amitabha's heart in the form of red or pink light, connecting with every living being in the universe.

If this visualisation does not come easily for you, an alternative form is to imagine a red rose at the centre of your heart, slowly opening and radiating soft red or pink light throughout every part of your body. Then you can visualise this light as a sphere gradually expanding beyond your body, again making a connection with every living being.

It is very good if you can hold this visualisation clearly in your mind, strengthening it with repeated practice. You should visualise this every day, as often as you can, over and over, until you become so familiar with it that you can feel the presence of Amitabha. It is important to feel a closeness or strong sense of connection with Amitabha. If you find this visualisation challenging, however, then just fill your mind with his ruby-red colour and his extraordinary love and compassion toward yourself and all beings. One final point is that when we visualise we are not just making something up, as when we imagine a piece of wood turning into gold; rather, we are trying to get in touch with a deeper reality.

It is also good to familiarise ourselves with some of the unique features of Sukhavati,[45] which are described in great detail in various

Buddhist texts. As I have mentioned before, there is no opportunity at all for mental afflictions to arise because the environment and its inhabitants are of such a pure nature.

3. Accumulation of Merit

You must also try as much as you can to perform good deeds and develop wholesome mental qualities. Be kind to others, avoid anger and jealousy, and learn to forgive and let go of anything to which you are attached. Remind yourself that you are trying to transform your mind so you can be reborn in Sukhavati. Also, pray that you will be reborn there for the benefit of all living beings, because when you are reborn there you will have much more freedom and ability to benefit others, possessing certain divine powers which are beyond our usual understanding. Cultivate merit and good actions through-out the day and avoid negative deeds. Each morning, check your motivation, making a decision to be kind and compassionate rather than motivated by self-interest. Resolve not to waste the day, but to use it wisely to accumulate merit with the aspiration of being reborn in Sukhavati. Each evening, reflect on your actions. Be aware of both your wholesome and unwholesome actions, dedicate and rejoice in your good deeds, and resolve never to repeat your negative actions in the future.

4. Dedication

You should dedicate whatever good you have performed throughout your life, as well as the oceans of good deeds performed by others that you know of or can imagine, towards taking a heavenly rebirth. Dedicating others' good deeds in addition to our own increases the strength of our aspiration. Whenever you perform a good deed, dedicate this with a sincere prayer, making a heartfelt wish that you will be reborn in Sukhavati for the sake of others. Think to yourself, 'May I dedicate my virtues together with the virtues of all beings so

I may be reborn in Sukhavati to benefit all others. May I dedicate these virtues towards dispelling all obstacles to accomplishing this practice. May I also dedicate these virtues so that all beings will have the good fortune to meet with and practise these teachings'.

Make sure you do not dedicate your good deeds towards a future rebirth with good health, beauty, wealth, position and so on. These qualities are limited and will run out. If your dedication is towards rebirth in Sukhavati, you will discover these and many more boundless qualities which are truly beyond your imagination.

LIFE AFTER DEATH

What actually happens when we die if we have trained well in the Amitabha practice? The teachings speak of being miraculously born from a lotus flower and having an experience of merging with a warm, limitless light, seeing the face of Amitabha directly or feeling his loving presence. We may receive a prophecy of our own enlightenment, or be guided by enlightened beings towards our rebirth.

If we become familiar with and develop strong faith in Amitabha then we can see him directly before death, and this direct experience will completely take away our fear of dying. Though this may sound unbelievable it is not just superstition. In my province in Tibet, I knew people who once had a busy life with no time to focus on spiritual practice, but then later turned their focus to the Amitabha meditation. As they were approaching old age and death, many of them had visions of Amitabha and felt very joyful and secure. Each of them experienced a peaceful, fearless and painless death. I directly witnessed these happenings only a few years ago—it is not just a story.

Does all of this apply to western people? Certainly! Those who have undergone a near-death experience often speak of being drawn toward and then enveloped by light,[46] as well as a presence of unconditional love. I was particularly interested to read that Elizabeth Kubler-Ross,[47] famous for her work with dying people, describes a very similar experience in her autobiography shortly before her own death. She recalls leaving her body and seeing many incredibly beautiful lotus blossoms in front of her, also seeing a light and knowing that she had to make it through one particular enormous lotus flower and merge with the light and its loving presence. After this experience, she lost all her fear of death:

Dying is nothing to fear. It can be the most wonderful experience of your life. It all depends on how you have lived. [48]

This is similar in many ways to the experience of the Amitabha practitioners in Tibet. Although she did not mention seeing a ruby red being, it is not necessary that specific details be identical, because one's perception depends on how one's mind is trained. What is more crucial is that we recognise the need to live as a good human being with strong faith and compassion, gaining unshakeable confidence that we will have a peaceful and fearless death.

Even if we have not become so familiar with the Amitabha practice or simply cannot relate to it, we must remind ourselves that all spiritual teachings inform us of the possibility of life after death. In the Tibetan tradition, there is much evidence to suggest this is not just a belief based on blind faith. One of the most telling examples is the Dalai Lama, whose present incarnation is Tenzin Gyatso, also known as His Holiness the fourteenth Dalai Lama. He was recognised at an early age as the incarnation of the thirteenth Dalai Lama by a rigorous process of examination which included, among other things, testing whether he could recognise objects familiar to him in his previous life. In addition, he progressed at an unusually rapid rate in his studies compared to other monks, suggesting a large amount of innate 'spiritual ability'. Furthermore, at the end of each lifetime, His Holiness gives an indication of where he will be reborn in his next life, suggesting that he has enough control over his mind to actually choose the circumstances of his rebirth, and that his deep commitment to the welfare of the Tibetan people is a pledge intended to last many lifetimes.

Similarly, there are many cases of Tibetan tulkus, or recognised reincarnations, who choose to come back lifetime after lifetime to continue the work at their monastery or even abroad, whatever their aspirations may be. Not only are they recognised by specific tests and the careful interpretation of 'signs', but many of them also have the ability to recollect key events of their past lives, in the same way that we may remember things that happened to us during our childhood.

This phenomenon is definitely not just limited to Tibetans. In recent times, quite a few westerners have been recognised as reincarnations of Tibetan lamas.[49] There are also now an impressive number of case reports of people from western countries with remarkable abilities to recollect what appear to be previous lives. Some of their stories correlate almost exactly with historical evidence from a particular era or a specific situation, revealing facts that simply could not have been gathered by fraudulent means. For example, there are many documented cases of young children who could identify houses and family members from their previous life,[50] remembering names and incidents which were confirmed by those still living in these places.

Basically, there are two types of rebirth. Firstly, there is rebirth by choice, where we can control our minds to a high degree and be reborn among people or situations where we can help others effectively, just like His Holiness the Dalai Lama. Then there is rebirth under the control of karma, in which case we are swept along by the power of our previous actions to a new existence, as determined by our emotions and karma.

To be reborn in Sukhavati, however, allows us to bypass this karmic chain reaction. It means we will never again be reborn in the human realm, or in any other realm, unless we choose to. This teaching is therefore extremely precious, as it can help us escape the cycle of uncontrolled death and rebirth once and for all.

Epilogue

This book has not been written just for the purpose of entertainment. Rather, it is my sincere wish that you will see it as a useful reference to which you can turn at any stage of life. I hope you will make use of it when you are facing difficulties, when you have big decisions to make, or when you just feel like taking some time out to reflect on how your life is going.

For this reason I strongly encourage you to not just place it on a bookshelf to gather dust when you have finished reading it. Keep it with you wherever you are. Reflect on its contents again and again, and apply the wisdom you gain to your everyday life. Discuss the ideas in this book with your partner, family or friends. Don't just accept them with blind faith but test them and see if they work for you, just like a scientist performing an experiment. Also, don't think that some sections are quite obvious and not worth reflecting upon, as we often struggle in certain areas of our life precisely because we fail to reflect on seemingly obvious things.

It will be most helpful if you can apply all the principles you learn to every situation you are confronted with, and then ask yourself how well this worked and whether you could do better next time. Keep doing this again and again, and renew your commitment to practising wholesome qualities every day, especially kindness and gratitude. Even if certain ideas seem obvious, remember there is a huge gap between knowing something and truly understanding or embodying it. Perhaps you can make space for fifteen to twenty minutes each day to begin a ritual of self-reflection, or even more regularly throughout the day— you will then be able to internalise the wisdom in this book and apply it to every situation in which you find yourself. Once you become proficient at practising wholesome mental qualities on a regular basis, you will gradually be able to experience the supreme joy which comes with the deeper levels of happiness.

As children, we want to feel good and confident in ourselves. As teenagers and young adults, we want to know the secrets of successful careers and relationships. As we grow older we want to learn how to live a rich and rewarding life, coping with changes and challenges in the best possible way. Finally, as we approach the end of our lives, we want to know how to prepare for a peaceful death. At each of these stages, we can learn to identify and cultivate the conditions which lead to happiness as they apply to our particular situation.

However, you should not think that only the chapter dedicated to your age group applies to you. It is possible that even if you are old and retired, you may find the teenage or young adult chapter most relevant to your life situation. On the other hand, even if you are young, you may find the later chapters of the book will help you greatly in preparing for your future, giving you some idea of how to deal with the challenges you encounter. Therefore, any chapter could be helpful for you at any time.

Imagine that some time in the future you are well-loved and respected by your local community. You are wise, generous and full of confidence; you are able to bring great benefit to the people around you, and every moment of your life is filled with true contentment and happiness. At least from the Buddhist point of view, this is how your life will become if you start cultivating the causes of happiness now, whether this be later on in this life or in a future life. As the Buddha said, 'What you are is what you have done, what you will be is what you do now'. From this perspective, we could think of this book as a guide to achieving happiness over many lifetimes, not just this life. So if you made a few bad decisions as a teenager, maybe next time round you will be a little wiser!

For many years I wished to write a book like this, as I realised how helpful it could have been when I was growing up. I also recognised that many of the issues I faced in Tibet were exactly the same as those that western people face, and that the causes of happiness are also identical, regardless of where we come from, how old we are or how much wealth we possess. Also, I have found that in the West we have an education system that puts great emphasis on being intelligent, knowledgeable and productive, yet there is little emphasis on learning how to deal with emotions and make wise decisions; this is often left to chance. Furthermore, it seems that there is not so much of a 'wisdom culture' nowadays, and people rarely have the opportunity to discuss life's big questions. I am hoping that this book will make a small contribution to closing some of these gaps.

There are now three final pieces of advice that I wish to leave you with. Firstly, I urge you never to seek happiness at the expense of other people. Secondly, I urge you to try as much as you can to bring benefit to others. Finally, I ask you to remember that happiness is almost always completely up to you and always depends on how much gratitude and appreciation you have in your heart. My heartfelt wish is that you will understand deeply the meaning of this book and be inspired to make the most of this precious human life. I pray that it will help guide you towards a rich, meaningful and happier life.

Recap of Exercises

THE BASIC MEDITATION METHOD

All types of meditation follow the same basic method, and this begins by consciously relaxing the body. A good way to achieve this is to do some gentle 'loosening exercises' prior to meditating, such as shaking or massaging different parts of your body or performing gentle yoga stretches. You should then consciously drop all concerns about the past and future, resolving to become someone with 'no history' while you are meditating. Focus your mind on awareness of the present moment, including your breath, the physical presence of your body, the sensations in your body, the sounds around you and the state of your mind, noticing how all these things arise and pass away.

Once your mindfulness is well established, you can continue to focus on the present moment, anchored by the awareness of breathing through your entire body (and knowing whether you are breathing a long breath or a short breath). Alternatively, you can shift your awareness towards a specific meditation object such as a visualisation, a sound, contemplation of a topic such as loving kindness or pure awareness of the breath at your heart or the tip of your nose.

It is inevitable that thoughts will arise, and you should just watch or notice these with the 'awareness aspect' of your mind without grasping at them, then gently return to the meditation object. Sounds and other sensations will still be there in the background; part of your mind will be aware of these sensations, yet they do not have to disturb your mindfulness if you can simply watch them without reacting. By practising in this way you should eventually arrive at a state where the body is relaxed, the emotions are calm and the mind is clear.

At first short, frequent sessions are the best way to develop a calm and balanced state of mind. That way, the practice will be enjoyable and interesting and you will be sure to notice a difference after doing it for some time. A calm state of mind will allow you to really feel the effect of the two practices that follow and gain real insight into their true meaning.

REFLECTION—MAKING DECISIONS

Think of any big decisions you have made recently. How did you make them? Did you ask other people who have plenty of life experience for advice? Did you thoroughly consider all the consequences of your decision? Were your expectations realistic or unrealistic? Did you consider the worst case scenario? Did you have any back-up plans? Were you completely honest with yourself, or did you make the decision because you wanted to impress someone? Did you consider all possible options?

Now think of any decisions you are about to make. Again think about all these things, making sure you consider all your options carefully. Now sit upright with your spine straight, relax your body, take a few big deep breaths and make your mind clear. If you are honest with yourself, what is the best decision?

EXERCISE—REFLECTING ON YOUR DAY

Set aside about fifteen minutes each morning and each evening. Each morning, check your attitude before starting the day. Did you appreciate that you were alive this morning, living in a country where the conditions make it so easy to live? Are you determined to use this day wisely and practise compassion whenever you can, being true to your deepest values? In your work and your relationships, are you willing to be patient if things don't work out the way you expect?

In the evening, reflect upon the day that has just passed. Think of the people you talked to, the places you visited and both the good and bad things that happened. What can you be grateful for? You may like to write a list of five to ten things in a 'gratitude journal'.

Sit up with your back straight, relax all your muscles and take a few big deep breaths. Try to rest in a natural feeling of contentment and joy and think about how you can make the next day truly meaningful and worthwhile.

EXERCISE—LEARNING FROM LIFE EXPERIENCE

We have accumulated much in the way of life experience now and can learn many valuable lessons if we reflect deeply on what our lives have taught us. This may even make us re-evaluate some of our priorities.

First bring to mind a person you had a relationship with in the past. This does not necessarily have to be a partner—it can be a friend, a parent or perhaps someone at work. What was your motivation for being in the relationship? Did it work out the way you expected? How successful were you at overcoming difficulties? How open was your communication? Perhaps if there was a period of great difficulty you can write down what you remember—this can help you accept the past and move on.

Then bring to mind a job you have had in the past and ask yourself similar questions. What was your motivation for doing this kind of work? What else did you learn from your experiences?

Now look at your present situation. Ask yourself, 'How can I apply the lessons I have learnt? How can I live my life in the wisest possible way?'

Sit upright with your spine straight and your hands in your lap, tensing your body and then feeling it relax all over. Ask yourself honestly if there is anything you want to change at this stage of your life, and then think about how you can make this happen.

EXERCISE—REFLECTING ON IMPERMANENCE

Bring to mind some of the losses and changes you have experienced by this time in your life, and contemplate the following thoughts:

- Whatever is born will get old and die.
- What has been gathered will be dispersed.
- What has been accumulated will be exhausted.
- What has been built up will collapse.

Friendship and enmity, fortune and sorrow, all the thoughts that run through our mind—everything is always changing.

Remind yourself that impermanence is simply the truth of how life is, and therefore the only thing we really have is now, the present. How could this understanding help you cope with the loss of a loved one? How could it change your perspective on the different types of losses that we face—the loss of dear ones, the loss of a job, the loss of anything we hold dear? It may also help to remember that changes do not necessarily lead to misfortune—sometimes they may benefit you greatly, even though this may not be apparent at first.

Reflecting on all these questions, sit with your back straight, feel your body relax and take a few big, gentle breaths. What lessons does the truth of impermanence hold for you?

Notes

CHAPTER 1: AN INTRODUCTION TO HAPPINESS

1. For a simple presentation of the Buddhist concept of enlightenment and how we can follow the path to enlightenment, refer to: Shar Khentrul Jamphel Lodrö, Unveiling Your Sacred Truth: A Gradual Discovery of Enlightenment through the Jonang-Shambala Kalachakra Tradition (Melbourne: Tibetan Buddhist Rimé Institute 2015).

2. See: Martin Seligman, Authentic happiness (Sydney: Random House, 2002).

3. The question of a 'happiness set point' was a major theme addressed at a conference between western scientists and the Dalai Lama in late 2004 which addressed the exciting new field of 'neuroplasticity', compiled in: Sharon Begley (ed), Train Your Mind, Change Your Brain (New York: Ballantine Books, 2007), 226-9. This issue is also discussed in: Norman Doidge. The Brain that Changes Itself (New York: Viking, 2007).

4. Several perspectives on happiness from western philosophers are beautifully described in layman's terms in: Alain de Botton, Consolations of Philosophy (London: Penguin Books, 2001).

5. A practical guide to cognitive therapy can be found in: David Burns, Feeling Good: the New Mood Therapy (New York: Avon Books, 1999).

6. See: P. Brickman, D. Coates and R. Janoff-Bulman, 'Lottery winners and accident victims: is happiness relative?' Journal of Personal and Social Psychology 36 (1978): 917-27.

7. See: T. Elbert, C. Pantev, C. Wienbruch, B. Rockstroh, and E. Taub, 'Increased cortical representation of the fingers of the left hand in string players,' Science 270 (1995): 305-7.

8. See: A. Lutz, L.L. Greischar, N.B. Rawlings, M. Ricard, and R.J. Davidson, 'Long-term meditators self-induce high-amplitude gamma synchrony during mental practice,' Proceedings of the National Academy of Sciences 101 (2004): 16369-73

9. See again: Sharon Begley (ed), Train Your Mind, Change Your Brain: 226-9.

CHAPTER 2: EXPLORING THE CONDITIONS OF HAPPINESS

10. The phenomenon of 'flow' has been well researched by psychologists—see: M. Csikszentmihalhyi, Finding Flow: The Psychology of Engagement with Everyday Life (Basic Books: 1998). From a Buddhist point of view, this is similar to attaining a state of single-pointed concentration – although this is a happy and blissful state of mind, it does not equate to the deepest level of happiness.

11. The field of positive psychology lists six key virtues or strengths which were found to be common to almost every tradition: wisdom, courage, love and humanity, justice, temperance and transcendence (or spirituality). Working to improve a person's virtuous qualities is now being seen as an important form of psychotherapy. See: Martin Seligman, Authentic happiness: 125-61.

12. See: Tal Ben-Shahar, Even Happier: A Gratitude Journal for Daily Joy and Lasting Fulfillment (New York: McGraw-Hill, 2010): 9-11.

13. This is the basic principle of a form of psychotherapy known as ACT (Acceptance and Commitment Therapy). It uses mindfulness tasks to directly tackle the problem of experiential avoidance, where we

compound our suffering by struggling with unwanted thoughts and feelings and reliving painful events. At the same time we focus on creating a fulfilling and rich life. Although reducing a patient's symptoms is not the goal of therapy, they are nearly always reduced as a by-product. See: Russel Harris, 'Embracing Your Demons: an Overview of Acceptance and Commitment Therapy.' Psychotherapy in Australia 12 (4): 2-8.

14. The approach of gaining awareness or insight into our negative tendencies has been the mainstay of western psychotherapy for many years. Cognitive therapy seeks to help us identify our moment to moment thinking patterns and then search for hidden assumptions that underlie these thoughts. Psychoanalysis, on the other hand, speaks about 'defence mechanisms' such as denial, repression or acting out, which block out painful past experiences; awareness and insight into these patterns can help us accept the past and move on.

CHAPTER 3: CHILDHOOD — SOWING THE SEEDS OF HAPPINESS

15. Modern psychology supports the view that parents have a crucial role in planting seeds in the minds of their children, even without them knowing it. It has even been said that children can 'tape' parental messages or that parents can hypnotise their child (see: Steve Biddulph, The Complete Secrets of Happy Children [Sydney: Harper Collins, 1998]). It is hoped that discussing important issues such as those raised in these stories will help create a family environment which is conducive to children receiving positive messages.

16. The Story of Friendship and The Story of Awareness are both adapted from stories from the life of the Buddha as presented in: Tich Nhat Hanh, Old Path White Clouds: Walking in the Footsteps of the Buddha. (Berkley: Parallax Press, 1991).

CHAPTER 4: TEENAGERS — SETTING OUT IN THE RIGHT DIRECTION

17. Tal Ben-Sahar speaks of three crucial things to consider when choosing a career or committing to any type of goal—strengths, pleasure and meaning. We should ask ourselves: 'What are our strengths?' 'What gives us pleasure?' and 'What gives us meaning?' He also suggests writing down what you really would like to do (something which comes from a deep sense of personal conviction or strong interest), and then checking if this is influenced in any way by the expectations of others. If you really want to do something, it doesn't ultimately matter what others think. See: Tal Ben-Shahar, Happier: Learn the Secrets to Daily Joy and Lasting Fulfillment (New York: McGraw Hill, 2007): 103-105.

18. In the Buddhist tantric tradition we speak of a dynamic psychophysical system within our bodies, which can be perceived directly after many years of yogic training. If we think of the human body as a city, then the channels are its roads, the inner air is like a horse and the mind is like its rider (visualised as subtle essences at particular locations in the body). For a more detailed explanation see: Sogyal Rinpoche, The Tibetan Book of Living and Dying (Sydney: Random House, 2002), 252-3.

CHAPTER 5: YOUNG ADULTHOOD — A SECOND CHANCE TO DEVELOP WISDOM

19. Modern psychology also agrees that it is crucial to have a mature view of romantic love. See: Tal Ben-Shahar, Happier: Learn the Secrets to Daily Joy and Lasting Fulfillment (111-22).

20. The degree of emotional intelligence that couples have is a key factor in keeping them together and strengthening their relationship, and according to John Gottman this is a skill which can be

learnt. This includes: learning to focus on each other's positive qualities, interacting frequently and openly, sharing values and interests and solving conflicts in a mature way, always being prepared to compromise. See: John Gottman & Nan Silver. The Seven Principles for Making Marriage Work (New York: Random House, 2000). For a practical guide to emotional intelligence see also: Jeanne Segal. The Language of Emotional Intelligence: The Five Essential Tools for Building Powerful and Effective Relationships (New York: McGraw Hill, 2008).

21. There are many studies now in the emerging field of mind-body medicine which look at the link between a peaceful mind and a healthy body. For a practical discussion on the relationship between stress and disease states see: Craig Hassed, Know Thyself: the Stress Relief Program. (Melbourne: Michelle Anderson Publishing, 2006, 18-22), and references therein.

22. In the Tibetan Buddhist tradition the highest form of compassion is known as bodhicitta, the altruistic wish to attain enlightenment in order to lead all living beings to enlightenment. See also: Shar Khentrul Jamphel Lodrö, Unveiling Your Sacred Truth.

23. From the Digha Nikaya, the Long Discourses of the Buddha (DN 31).

CHAPTER 6: MIDLIFE — THE AGE OF EXPERIENCE

24. The Noble Eightfold Path includes: right view, right intention, right action, right speech, right livelihood, right effort, right concentration and right mindfulness. The first two stages represent wisdom, the following four represent discipline and the final two are to do with concentration. There are many different approaches to understanding the Buddhist teachings. A good

introductory perspective is given by: Walpola Rahula, What the Buddha Taught. (London: Gordon Fraser, 1978). For a description of the stages on the path to enlightenment see: Shar Khentrul Jamphel Lodrö, Unveiling Your Sacred Truth.

25. There are many accounts of the incredible life of the 16th Karmapa. See, for example: Ken Holmes, Karmapa (Forres: Altea Publishing, 1995). I also mention my own root master Kyabje Lobsang Trinley, whose tireless dedication for the benefit of others, as well as many miraculous signs during his life and his death, I personally witnessed.

26. For guidelines on how to find and follow an authentic spiritual teacher, see, for example: His Holiness the Dalai Lama. Becoming Enlightened (New York: Atria Books, 2009), 31-36. For an in-depth discussion see also Shar Khentrul Jamphel Lodrö, Unveiling Your Sacred Truth.

27. From the Digha Nikaya, the Long Discourses of the Buddha (DN 31). In this sutta the Buddha discusses the ethics and practices of lay followers.

28. It is common knowledge in western psychology that men and women see the world in subtly different ways: The examples given here are based on: John Gray, Men are from Mars, Women are from Venus: the Classic Guide to Understanding the Opposite Sex (New York: Harper Collins, 2004).

29. An excellent reference for parents, which tallies with many of the ideas presented here, is: Steve Biddulph, The Complete Secrets of Happy Children (Sydney: Harper Collins, 1998).

30. In modern psychology a key principle in achieving happiness at work is to craft one's work into a 'calling'. We can identify what we find meaningful and what our strengths are, and then learn

to perceive work in a way that is personally meaningful, while at the same time focusing on our strengths or good qualities. See: Martin Seligman, Authentic Happiness, 165-184.

CHAPTER 7: MATURE ADULTHOOD — THE AGE OF WISDOM

31. For an in-depth discussion and reflection on death and impermanence from a Buddhist point of view, see: Shar Khentrul Jamphel Lodrö, Unveiling Your Sacred Truth.

32. This is the story of Krisha Gotami, as recounted in: Sogyal Rinpoche, The Tibetan Book of Living and Dying, 28-9.

33. We may choose a spiritual tradition or community to help us cultivate our 'inner life' and good qualities, yet we can also find help in certain practical books or courses in psychology (so long as they have a sound research basis). A good example of such a book is: Tal Ben-Shahar, Even Happier: A Gratitude Journal for Daily Joy and Lasting Fulfillment (New York: McGraw-Hill, 2010).

34. See: Sharon Begley, Train Your Mind, Change Your Brain, 246-9 (and references therein). See also: Norman Doidge, The Brain that Changes Itself. Nowadays there are a number of good practical books and other resources which can help us improve our memory. One such resource is the website www.lumosity.com, which provides on-line exercises which target improving different areas of mental function, backed up by good scientific research. Another useful resource, which may benefit people at any age, is: Tony Buzan, Use Your Head: Innovative Learning and Thinking Techniques to fulfill your Mental Potential (Harlow: Educational Publishers LLP, 2006).

35. For a discussion of the benefits of developing gratitude, from the perspective of modern psychology, see: Martin Seligman, Authentic Happiness, 70-5.

CHAPTER 8: LATE ADULTHOOD — DEPARTURE FROM THIS LIFE

36. For an in-depth discussion of the Buddhist view of karma and reincarnation, including a logical 'proof' of both of these principles, see: Shar Khentrul Jamphel Lodrö, Unveiling Your Sacred Truth.

37. Much research has been done on the psychological benefits of helping others; for example, doing volunteer work can help lower levels of depression and anxiety, and helping others abstain from alcohol can help prevent relapse in former alcoholics. Much of this research is presented in: Stephen Post, Why Good Things Happen to Good People (New York: Broadway, 2007).

38. For an in-depth presentation of the traditional Buddhist view of suffering, see: Shar Khentrul Jamphel Lodrö, Unveiling Your Sacred Truth.

39. For an in-depth discussion of the stages we go through when faced with the diagnosis of a terminal illness, see: Elizabeth Kubler-Ross, On Death and Dying (London: Tavistock/Routledge, 1989). Kubler-Ross's research was based on an extensive series of interviews with dying patients, transcripts of which appear in her book.

40. For a more detailed account of the outer and inner dissolution process at the moment of death, according to the Tibetan Buddhist tradition, see: Sogyal Rinpoche, The Tibetan Book of Living and Dying, 255-260. See also: Shar Khentrul Jamphel Lodrö, Unveiling Your Sacred Truth.

41. One of the greatest Tibetan masters of the last generation, the 16th Karmapa died in a western hospital in the United States in 1981. Some of the remarkable details of his death, including an account by one of his attending doctors, are recounted in: Reginald Ray, Secret of the Vajra World (Boston: Shambala, 2001), p465-80.

42. The transition period or intermediate state between death and rebirth in a new body is mapped out in considerable detail in the Tibetan Buddhist tradition. See: Sogyal Rinpoche, The Tibetan Book of Living and Dying, p291–302. For a more detailed description see: Shar Khentrul Jamphel Lodrö, Unveiling Your Sacred Truth.

43. A useful reference book for those wishing to begin and sustain a meditation practice is: Graham Williams, Life in Balance: the Life-flow Guide to Meditation (Adelaide: Print Know How 2008). Other good references include: Ajahn Brahm, Mindfulness, Bliss and Beyond: A Meditator's Handbook (Somerville: Wisdom 2006) and B. Alan Wallace, The Attention Revolution: Unlocking the Power of the Focused Mind (Boston: Wisdom 2006). See also: Shar Khentrul Jamphel Lodrö, Unveiling Your Sacred Truth.

44. More complete details of the traditional Vajrasattva purification practice can be found in chapter sixteen of: Shar Khentrul Jamphel Lodrö, Unveiling Your Sacred Truth.

45. There are numerous Buddhist texts which speak about Amitabha pure land practice and features of Sukhavati, which you may wish to research; some of these are actually based on the direct visions of highly realised masters. One of the most precious texts was composed by the nineteenth century lama Tsoknyi Gyamtso, and consists of over one hundred pages of Tibetan text describing this pure realm. It is my deep wish to translate this text in the near future and make it widely available.

46. For research into the near-death experience see, for example: Kenneth Ring, Life at Death: a Scientific Investigation of the Near-death Experience (Boston: Arkana 1985).

47. Elizabeth Kubler-Ross, A Memoir of Living and Dying: The Wheel of Life (London: Bantam 1997).

48. Elizabeth Kubler- Ross, The Wheel of Life, p288.

49. In recent times a few westerners have been recognised as reincarnations: See: Vickie MacKenzie, Reborn in the West: the Reincarnation Masters (London: Bloomsbury 1995).

50. Over many years, Dr Ian Stevenson has collected detailed evidence for over two thousand cases of children recalling previous lives. See: Ian Stevenson, Twenty Cases Suggestive of Reincarnation (Charlottesville: Univ. of Virginia Press, 1974); and Jane Henry (ed), Parapsychology Research on Exceptional Experiences (London: Routledge 2005). Unfortunately such research is often dismissed because it is not considered 'mainstream'—however, I believe it would benefit us greatly to evaluate it with a critical yet open mind, as we would in 'mainstream' science.

Resources

PRACTICAL BOOKS BASED ON MODERN PSYCHOLOGY

Tal Ben-Shahar. Even Happier: A Gratitude Journal for Daily Joy and Lasting Fulfillment (New York: McGraw-Hill, 2010).

Tal Ben-Shahar. Happier: Learn the Secrets to Daily Joy and Lasting Fulfillment (New York: McGraw-Hill, 2007).

Steve Biddulph. The Complete Secrets of Happy Children (Sydney: Harper Collins,1998).

John Bradshaw. Healing the Shame that Binds You (Deerfield Beach: Health Communications, 1988).

David Burns. Feeling Good: the New Mood Therapy (New York: Avon Books, 1999).

John Gottman & Nan Silver. The Seven Principles for Making Marriage Work (New York: Random House, 2000).

Russ Harris. The Happiness Trap: Stop Struggling, Start Living (Wollombi: Exisle Publishing, 2007).

Craig Hassed. Know Thyself: the Stress Relief Program (Melbourne: Michelle Anderson Publishing, 2006).

Jeanne Segal. The Language of Emotional Intelligence: The Five

Essential Tools for Building Powerful and Effective Relationships (New York: McGraw Hill, 2008).

Martin Seligman. Authentic Happiness (Sydney: Random House, 2002).

Timothy Sharp. The Happiness Handbook (Sydney: Finch, 2007).

INFORMATION ON THE SPIRITUAL LIFE (FROM A BUDDHIST PERSPECTIVE)

Bikkhu Bodhi (ed). In the Buddha's Words: An Anthology of Discourses from the Pali Canon (Boston: Wisdom 2005).

Ajahn Chah. A Still Forest Pool: The Insight Meditation of Ajahn Chah. Compiled by Jack Kornfield and Paul Breiter (New York: Quest, 1986).

His Holiness the Dalai Lama. Becoming Enlightened (New York: Atria Books, 2009).

His Holiness the Dalai Lama. How to Practise: The Way to a Meaningful Life (Rider: London, 2002).

Philip Kapleau. The Three Pillars of Zen: Teaching, Practice and Enlightenment (Anchor Books: New York, 2000).

Walpola Rahula, What the Buddha Taught. (London: Gordon Fraser, 1978).

Shar Khentrul Rinpoche Jamphel Lodro, A Secret Incarnation: Reflections on the Life of a Tibetan Lama. (Melbourne: TBRI 2014)

Shar Khentrul Rinpoche Jamphel Lodro. Unveiling Your Sacred Truth: A Gradual Discovery of Enlightenment through the Jonang-Shambala Kalachakra Tradition. (Melbourne: TBRI 2014)

About the Author

Khentrul Rinpoche is a Non-Sectarian Master of Tibetan Buddhism. He has devoted his life to a wide variety of spiritual practices, studying with more than 25 masters from all of the major Tibetan traditions. While he has genuine respect and appreciation for all spiritual systems, he has the greatest confidence and experience with his personal path of the *Kalachakra Tantra* as taught in the *Jonang-Shambhala Tradition*.

Rinpoche brings a sharp and inquisitive mind to everything that he does. His teachings are both accessible and direct, often emphasising a very pragmatic sensibility. Over the years, Rinpoche has authored a variety of books to guide his students. He has specifically made great efforts to translate and provide commentary on texts which present the gradual stages of the *Kalachakra Path*.

Rinpoche believes that our world definitely has the potential to develop genuine peace and harmony while still preserving our environment and humanity. This *Golden Age of Shambhala* is possible through the study and practice of the Kalachakra System. To this end, Rinpoche has begun travelling the world to share his knowledge of this unique lineage free from sectarian bias.

Rinpoche's Vision

The *Tibetan Buddhist Rimé Institute* was founded with the express purpose of supporting Khentrul Rinpoche in realising his vision for greater peace and harmony in this world. As our community continues to grow and develop, more and more people are getting involved with this extraordinary effort.

To give you a sense of the scope of Rinpoche's vision, we can speak of eight goals that reflect Rinpoche's short and long term priorities:

IMMEDIATE GOALS

Ultimately speaking, lasting, genuine happiness is only possible through profound personal transformation. Now more than ever, we need methods to develop our wisdom and actualise our greatest potential. It is for this reason that Rinpoche places such a heavy priority on the preservation of the Jonang Kalachakra Lineage. There are four ways in which Rinpoche proposes to do this:

1. **Create opportunities to connect with an authentic and complete Kalachakra lineage in close collaboration with dedicated meditators in remote Tibet.** Our goal is to create all of the supports for practicing Kalachakra in accordance with the authentic lineage masters who have upheld this tradition for thousands of years. We do this by commissioning statues and paintings, writing books and giving teachings around the world. We place particular emphasis on ensuring the authenticity of our materials, drawing on the profound experience of highly realised meditators who are dedicating their lives to these practices.

2. **Establish international retreat centres for the study and practice of Kalachakra.** In order to integrate the teachings into our minds, it is crucial to have the opportunity to engage in periods of intensive practice. Therefore, we are working to create the necessary infrastructure that will support and nurture the members of our community to engage in both short and long-term retreat. This includes the purchase of land and the construction of everything that is needed to conduct group and solitary retreats. Our long-term aim is to develop a network of such centres around the world, forming a global community that supports a wide variety of practitioners.

3. **Translate and publish the unique and rare texts of Kalachakra masters.** The Kalachakra System has been the subject of countless texts over the course of Tibet's long history. So far, only a small fraction of these texts have been translated and made accessible in the West. While the theoretical texts are important, we aim to focus particularly on the pith instructions that will guide dedicated practitioners to a deeper experience of these profound teachings.

4. **Develop the tools and programs for a structured learning experience.** With pockets of students distributed throughout the world, we believe it is important to make the most of modern technologies to facilitate the process of learning for our students. Our aim is to develop a robust online educational platform that allows our international community to access quality study programs that are intuitive, structured and engaging.

LONG-TERM GOALS

While we each work towards achieving ultimate peace and harmony in our own minds, we must not lose sight of the fact that we exist within the context of a world filled with a great diversity of individuals. These individuals give rise to a wide variety of beliefs and practices that in turn shape how we relate and interact with each other. In this interdependent reality, it is vital to find viable strategies for promoting greater tolerance and respect. To this end, Rinpoche proposes four specific areas of activity:

1. **Promote the development of a Rimé Philosophy through dialogue with other traditions.** With the desire to be constructive members of a pluralistic society, we need to learn ways of reconciling our differences. To this end, we aim to help people develop the positive qualities that promote an attitude of mutual respect, openness to new ideas and an inquisitive desire to overcome our ignorance.

2. **Develop highly realised role models by offering financial support to dedicated practitioners.** In order to ensure the authenticity of our spiritual traditions, it is imperative that there are people who actualise the highest of realisations. Therefore, we aim to create a financial scholarship program which facilitates genuine practitioners who wish to dedicate their lives to spiritual development, regardless of their system of practice. By helping people actualise the teachings, they become positive role models for those around them, inspiring and guiding the generations to come.

3. **Actualise the great potential of female practitioners by developing specialised training programs.** The Tibetan culture has a long history of cultivating highly realised masters through the intensive training of those who are recognised to have great potential. Unfortunately, all too often the search for potential was focused only on male candidates. Rinpoche believes that it is increasingly important to have strong, highly realised, female role models who can help to bring greater balance into our world. For this reason, we are working to develop a unique training program

for providing women with the opportunity to actualise their spiritual potential. It is our aim to design a specialised curriculum as well as the financial infrastructure to fully support all aspects of their education.

4. **Promote greater flexibility of mind and a broader understanding of reality through modern educational programs.** In a world that is rapidly evolving, we need to rethink the types of skills that we are teaching our children. The rigid structures of the past are often ill equipped to prepare students for the challenges that they will face during their lives. Therefore, we aim to develop a variety of educational programs that can help children to become more flexible and more capable of adapting to their context. An important part of these programs is the development of greater awareness of the role that our mind plays in our day-to-day experiences. We also aim to bring reforms into the monastic education system that would help make them more relevant for the modern world.

HOW CAN YOU HELP?

None of this will be possible without your support and participation. This vision will require a vast amount of merit and generosity from multiple benefactors over the course of many years. If you would like to help then please do not hesitate to contact us.

Tibetan Buddhist Rimé Institute
1584 Burwood Highway
Belgrave VIC 3160
AUSTRALIA

temple@rimebuddhism.com
www.rimebuddhism.com